The Great American
Wilderness
Touring America's
National Parks

2nd Edition

Larry H. Ludmer

HUNTER
PUBLISHING

Hunter Publishing, Inc.
300 Raritan Center Parkway
Edison NJ 08818, USA
Tel (908) 225 1900
Fax (908) 417 0482

164 Commander Boulevard
Agincourt, Ontario
CANADA M15 3C7
Tel (416) 293 8141

ISBN 1-55650-730-5

2nd Edition © 1996 Larry Ludmer

Maps by Joyce Huber, PhotoGraphics

Cover Photo: Grand Canyon
(Henryk Kaiser/Leo de Wys, Inc.)

Acknowledgements

I would like to express my thanks to Linda Meyers of the National Park Service Division of Publications, who was gracious in providing information on which the maps in this book are based.

Special thanks are also due to my mother, who so carefully helped to proofread the manuscript and, especially, to my brother, David. As my travel companion through the parks, he added immeasurably to this volume.

Other books by Larry Ludmer include:

Arizona, Utah, Colorado: A Touring Guide
1-55650-656-2, $11.95
Northern Rockies: A Touring Guide
1-55650-684-8, $11.95
Maine, New Hampshire & Vermont: A Touring Guide
1-55650-728-3, $10.95
Cruising Alaska, 2nd Ed.
1-55650-699-6, $11.95

Contents

Maps

Introduction

One of our greatest treasures is the diverse beauty that nature has bestowed upon the American landscape. While many parts of the world may contain majestic mountains, eye-popping geological phenomena, rushing waterfalls, and more, nowhere is there a greater variety or concentration of such wonders as in the United States. The very best of these have been set aside in parks, monuments, and other areas administered by the National Park Service. These are truly the crown jewels of America. They have been created to be seen, felt, touched and enjoyed by everyone.

And that is precisely what this book is about: seeing and enjoying nature at its most inspiring, its most unusual, and its most powerful. There are nearly 400 separate areas administered by the National Park Service. A great many of these have to do with people, places, or events that have played a significant role in the development of our nation. This book brings you only those parks that are especially worthwhile, regardless of how "popular" they are, and eliminates many heavily-visited areas whose primary attraction is miles of beachfront for frolicking in the ocean.

Equally important, this book assumes you will be visiting the parks by car. That eliminates some highly inaccessible locations, as well as much of the natural beauty in Alaska, since those areas are best seen on guided tours or via cruise ship.

Most of the existing works on our nation's scenic areas may describe park features in exquisite detail, but they don't really tell you how to see what has been described. A number of books are aimed at people who will be spending a great deal of time hiking and camping in the back-country. Admittedly, this is the best way to see what the parks have to offer, but the reality is that many thousands of people have neither the time nor the inclination to "rough it" in the wilderness; or they may have physical limitations due to age or other factors. The primary goal of the book is to help you make the most of your time in each park, detailing those highlights that should not be missed – even if you don't plan to spend days trekking through the back-country or hiding in a blind with binoculars in hand waiting for a rare bird to appear.

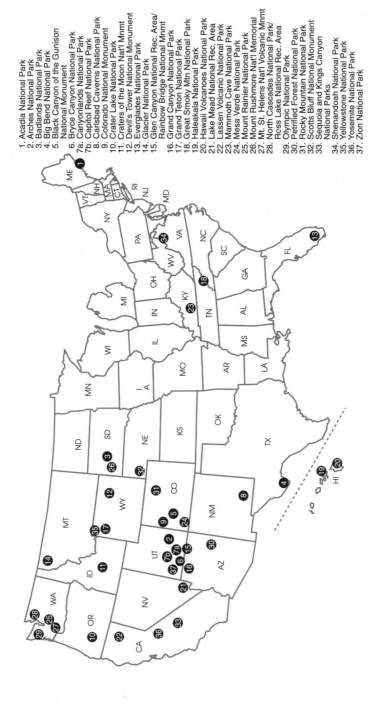

1. Acadia National Park
2. Arches National Park
3. Badlands National Park
4. Big Bend National Park
5. Black Canyon of the Gunison National Monument
6. Bryce Canyon National Park
7a. Canyonlands National Park
7b. Capitol Reef National Park
8. Carlsbad Caverns National Park
9. Colorado National Monument
10. Crater Lake National Park
11. Craters of the Moon Nat'l Mnmt
12. Devil's Tower National Monument
13. Everglades National Park
14. Glacier National Park
15. Glen Canyon National Rec. Area/ Rainbow Bridge National Mnmt
16. Grand Canyon National Park
17. Grand Teton National Park
18. Great Smoky Mtn National Park
19. Haleakala National Park
20. Hawaii Volcanoes National Park
21. Lake Mead National Rec. Area
22. Lassen Volcanic National Park
23. Mammoth Cave National Park
24. Mesa Verde National Park
25. Mount Rainier National Park
26. Mount Rushmore Nat'l Memorial
27. Mt. St. Helens Nat'l Volcanic Mnmt
28. North Cascades National Park/ Rcss Lake National Rec. Area
29. Olympic National Park
30. Petrified Forest National Park
31. Rocky Mountain National Park
32. Scotts Bluff National Monument
33. Sequoia and Kings Canyon National Parks
34. Shenandoah National Park
35. Yellowstone National Park
36. Yosemite National Park
37. Zion National Park

The National Park Service has designated the areas it administers as National Parks, National Monuments, Recreation Areas, and so forth. (Actually, Congress is the only body that can designate an area as a National Park.) Frequently, but not always, national parks are larger, more famous and have the greatest attraction for visitors. But there are a number of "non-park" areas that are every bit as worthwhile as any of the national parks. In this book, 41 separate areas are described in 37 chapters (some are so close geographically that they are commonly thought of together and are, therefore, discussed in pairs). Of these, 30 are national parks, seven are national monuments, three are national recreation areas, and one is a national memorial.

General Planning

Insufficient planning can lead to unfulfilled expectations and wasted time. Of course, some people like to do things on an *ad hoc* basis, and there is definitely something to be said for spontaneity. However, unless you have the extra time such unplanned trips can take, proper planning is essential. The longer the trip and the more you wish to accomplish during your vacation, the more this axiom applies.

Some of the major things that should be decided in advance are: What exactly do you want to see? How many miles are you willing to drive and how much time do you have to spend? What types of accommodations do you want?

The first and most important step in the planning process is to write down your proposed itinerary. Block off each day's activities by how long they will take. Be sure to allow enough time for driving, including rest and meal stops. Once your outline is in place, it is easy to make emendations. When you actually begin your trip, the itinerary is your travel guide. Adjustments can be made, of course, as you go along. Be sure to bring along materials on additional sights that may be visited should you be running ahead of schedule and have extra time on your hands. After all, why not put that time to good use?

The information in this book will enable you to create an itinerary for each park. This does not mean that you will not need or want other information. If you are a member of the American Automobile Association, their TourBooks might be of help to you. One source that is a natural partner to this book is the National Park

Service itself. Each park or area has a superintendent's office that will be most happy to furnish you with brochures. The information they send is generally clear, concise, and extremely useful. Moreover, most of their literature includes an excellent map of the park. While narrative description is important, a good map is absolutely indispensable, except perhaps for the smallest of our national parks. A map of each park is included in this book but, while these are a good starting point for your planning, they are no substitute for a detailed Park Service map. Make every effort to secure such a map before you depart. You will also need adequate maps of the areas that you will be covering en route to and from the parks. The AAA, again, can be an excellent source, or there are equally good maps to be found at gas stations and map stores. Do not rely on the small maps in most road atlases.

Many people like to have an informed commentary as they tour the parks. If you are one of them, you might want to consider an Auto Tape Tour. These can be rented or purchased at many of the larger national parks or you can get them in advance (purchase only). The company that specializes in such tapes is CC Inc., P.O. Box 385, Scarsdale, NY 10583. Tapes are not available for every area.

AAA and similar guidebooks have extensive listings on where to eat and where to stay overnight. This book will describe in-park accommodations as a convenience to the reader. The rating systems used by the various guides differ but, in general, you can rely on them to select places that won't bring any unpleasant surprises. Make advance reservations to avoid being stranded when the hotels are fully booked. This is especially important within the parks where hotels often have a limited number of rooms that are frequently booked far in advance. If the guidebook lists only local telephone numbers you might want to call the toll-free operator (1-800-555-1212) to find out if there is an 800 number available.

Using This Book

Each chapter begins with a brief narrative that introduces you to the park, including its outstanding features. It is meant to spark your interest rather than provide a comprehensive description.

FACTS AND FIGURES: This section is subdivided according to the following headings:

Location/Gateways/Getting There: Where the park is located and how to get there from the nearest large city or cities (which I refer to as the gateway). Abbreviations used include "I" for interstate highways, "US" for federal highways, and "SR" for state routes.

Admission Fees: The user fee per automobile (good for a period of one to three days, depending upon the area) will be listed. This fee applies regardless of the number of passengers. Rates for trailers, where allowed, will be higher. The Park Service provides three special forms of admission. One is the *Golden Age Passport*, available to any person over 62. It can be obtained from any National Park Service office upon presentation of proof of age and is good for a lifetime. The cost is $10. Besides admitting the senior citizen, anyone traveling in the same car will also be admitted at no additional charge. The *Golden Eagle Passport* is available for $25 to persons of any age and is good for one year from the date of issue. It also admits everyone traveling with the bearer in the same car. Certainly, if you are going to be visiting several park areas that have user fees, the Golden Eagle is well worth the small initial outlay. The *Golden Access Pass* is issued free of charge to any person who is disabled under federal program guidelines. All Passports are valid at all National Park Service "Fee Areas." The daily user fee and the Passports only admit you into the park. In most instances, tours and other special activities, whether conducted by the Park Service or a private concessionaire, will involve an additional charge. If this is the case, it is indicated by a dollar sign ($) in the text. However, Passes offer discounts on other activities if they are *not* run by a private concessionaire. In almost all cases, ranger-guided walks are free.

Climate/When to Go: Unless you are the hardy type interested in mushing through snow in the bitter cold, most of your visits will be in summer. In fact, a lot of the most scenic park roads are closed in winter. However, summer is not always the best time to visit. This section will give you information on climatic conditions in each park, along with road closings and the availability of services throughout the year.

Address/Telephone: In the past couple of years many of the parks have instituted automated information systems where you can call at any time and, using a touch-tone telephone, hear recorded information on topics you select. It is sometimes more difficult now to speak with a real live person!

AUTO TOUR/SHORT STOPS: This, along with the next section, forms the heart of each chapter. In this part the park roads and what can be seen from them will be described. There is information on short walks (those that can be accomplished in under 20 minutes, round-trip), visitor centers and museums, the best scenic over-looks, and more. A suggested minimum time allotment for the tour is given.

GETTING OUT/LONGER STOPS: Hopefully your visit will allow time for much more than just the Auto Tour and a few brief strolls. If it does, then refer to this section for useful descriptions of some longer walks that are well worth the time and effort they may require. Not included are any hikes that take more than half a day or that require unusual stamina or special skills, such as mountain climbing. I do assume that you will be capable of walking up to several miles on terrain that isn't always level and is, generally, unpaved. Remember that many parks are located in higher altitudes, which makes even an apparently simple walk somewhat more difficult.

SPECIAL ACTIVITIES: This section will only be found for those parks that have guided tours and other unusual activities that were not included in the preceding sections. Virtually all National Park Service areas in this book do offer nature walks, escorted hikes and campfire programs, all conducted by Park Rangers. Information on these activities can best be obtained either by writing for a listing and schedule or by inquiring at any visitor center upon arrival. Schedules often change from year to year and depending on the season.

ACCOMMODATIONS: In-park accommodations are briefly described and characterized as to type – motel, cabins, lodge. A price range is given as follows:

Budget (B)	Under $60 per night
Moderate (M)	Between $60 and $90
Expensive (E)	Over $90

All prices are for double occupancy. When two price ranges are shown it indicates that there is a wide variety of rooms available, with great differences as to quality. The price range is accurate at press time. Even with inflation, the category rating of a particular facility will usually remain valid. That is, a moderate-price facility will probably still be moderate in comparison to other places five years from now.

Campgrounds and trailer parking can be found in almost all of the areas, but they will not be described. You can write to the park for further information or look in one of the many good campground directories in bookstores. Keep in mind that hauling a trailer in the mountain parks can be impractical. In some cases, their use is heavily restricted. As for campgrounds, most are fully booked early in the travel season, so plan ahead. Campground reservations in many parks are handled by MISTIX. See "For More Information" section for contacts.

DINING: Information is limited to within-park facilities, though nearby towns offering food are given.

WHERE DO WE GO FROM HERE? This final section of each chapter references the *Suggested Trips* found in the last part of the book. These trips focus primarily on parks that are near one another and that can be combined as part of a single itinerary. Many of the outstanding non-park attractions to be found along the route are described here as well.

The National Parks

1

Acadia National Park

We'll begin our scenic journey with America's easternmost national park, Acadia. This area of Maine used to be a part of the French Province of Acadia, hence the name. Acadia offers majestic cliffs rising sharply from the ocean, with the surf constantly pounding at and eroding their bases. Within the park is the highest point on the Atlantic seaboard, Cadillac Mountain, which rises 1,530 feet. Besides the beautiful cliffs and scenic seacoast, it is an area of great diversity in vegetation. Many types of trees and flowers dot the interior.

Park land occupies the greater part of Mount Desert Island. Many smaller patches of land are, however, in private ownership and the landscape is thus dotted with picturesque towns jammed with fishing boats and recreational vessels. Take time to sample some of the many local seafood restaurants and other business establishments. When hiking, be sure that you are not violating private property.

Facts & Figures

LOCATION/GATEWAYS/GETTING THERE: Along the coast of north-central Maine, Acadia is about 5½ hours from Boston, taking

I-95 to Bangor and then proceeding 47 miles via US 1A and SR 3 to the town of Bar Harbor, gateway to the park.

YEAR ESTABLISHED: The island was first discovered by Champlain in 1604 and was settled about a decade later. It became a national park in 1919.

SIZE: 39,707 acres (or 62 square miles).

ADMISSION FEE: $5.

CLIMATE/WHEN TO GO: Acadia is open all year, but the Park Loop Road is closed in winter. Since spring and fall are a bit chilly for comfortable sightseeing, you should plan to visit during the summer months, even though it is much more crowded at this time. Crowds are at their peak in August, so June and July are the best months. If you don't mind the weather being somewhat brisk, fall can be a very beautiful time – generally dry, with the foliage putting on its annual display of color.

ADDRESS/TELEPHONE: Superintendent, Acadia National Park, P.O. Box 177, Bar Harbor, ME 04069. (207) 288-3338.

Auto Tour/Short Stops

The park is not one continuous stretch of land, but rather is in three separate sections – the largest and most important being Mount Desert Island, as well as Isle Au Haut (accessible only by boat), and the Schoodic Peninsula area, approximately 40 miles east of the main section. We'll consider Mount Desert Island first.

Entering the park via SR 3, you will soon reach the Hull's Cove Visitor Center where there are exhibits about the park and the history of the area, as well as information on activities within the park. Here, too, begins the 27-mile-long **Park Loop Road**, which passes many of the park's outstanding features. There are frequent turnouts for scenic views of the rocky coast. The road is one-way (south) for 20 miles from just below the Cadillac Mountain entrance to Seal Harbor.

About 10 miles south of the visitor center begins the primary concentration of scenic attractions along the Ocean Drive section of the Loop Road, and they will come upon you in rather quick succession, so drive slowly and be ready to stop.

Acadia National Park

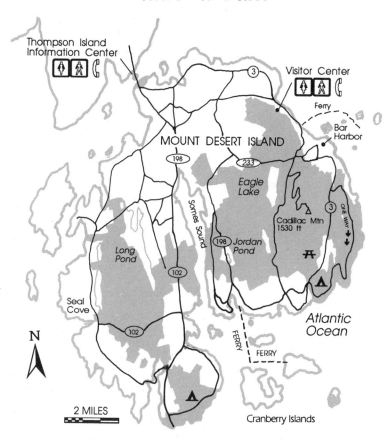

First is **Great Head**, one of the largest rock headlands on the east coast. Next is **Sand Beach**, composed almost entirely of millions of tiny sea shell fragments. Soon after is one of the most famous points in the park, the impressive **Thunder Hole**. Here, wave erosion has created a chasm that can, when wave and tide conditions are right, produce extremely loud reverberations that do, indeed, sound like thunder. Even when the conditions aren't just right, you are almost certain to encounter heavy surf crashing into the gorge – a very pretty picture. Finally, after Thunder Hole are the **Otter Cliffs**, where a heavily forested area extends right to the edge of the cliffs, more than one hundred feet above the Atlantic Ocean.

The Loop Road then skirts the south shore of the island before heading north. Several miles afterward you will reach a side road that leads to the summit of **Cadillac Mountain**. Be sure not to miss this short detour as there are fine views in all directions, but especially to the south and east where the terrain slopes sharply down to the sea.

A bit further north from Cadillac the Loop Road reaches its end. However, there is a second loop, via SRs 233, 198 and 102, that visits the southwestern portion of Mount Desert Island. Although this part of the park is not nearly as scenic as the area you just came from, it offers many picturesque seaside towns and coves.

The second loop leads you back into SR 3. The driving tour of Mount Desert Island (both loops) covers 50 miles and you should allow about three hours to complete it, including stops.

Should you wish to see the Schoodic Peninsula portion of the park, follow SR 3 into US 1 northbound and then SR 186. The main attraction is **Schoodic Point**, a rocky headland that rises more than 400 feet from the ocean. It provides outstanding vistas of the Bay of Fundy and the Mount Desert Mountains across Frenchman Bay. This addition to your route will take about 2½ hours, including the round-trip drive.

Getting Out/Longer Stops

The stops above are all just a short walk from the roadside parking areas. But the park contains many miles of trails. The easiest are the graded carriage roads, originally designed for horse-and-buggy travel (and a concession in the park still offers carriage rides – $). The carriage roads cross the park road at numerous locations and give you a chance to explore more of the park's interior with its lush pine forests and flowers. The same general type of landscape can be seen from the many hiking trails, but the carriage roads are improved – you can simply take a meandering journey over the gentle hills for as long as you like. Bar Harbor and Northeast Harbor have bike rental shops and this is another good way to explore the carriage roads.

Special Activities

There are several cruises that take visitors to islands off the coast and a number of these have commentary supplied by a park ranger ($). You can also take a **ferry** from Stonington ($), a town that is east of Mount Desert Island via SRs 176, 175 and 15, to **Isle Au Haut**. This tiny island has some very scenic ocean vistas, but the drive to Stonington is rather long and the scenery is not significantly different from that in other portions of the park.

Accommodations & Dining

The only place to eat within the park is the charming **Jordan Pond House**, set on the shore of the pond itself. There are no overnight facilities within the park's boundaries, but numerous establishments can be found in the towns of Bar Harbor and Northeast Harbor (both in the Mount Desert Island section). The former is especially noted for its variety of places to stay.

Where Do We Go From Here?

As Acadia is not near any other national park, it is not included in one of the itineraries at the end of the book. However, both the **White Mountains** of New Hampshire and the **Green Mountains** of Vermont are very beautiful and have enough points of interest to make them worthwhile vacation destinations. Large sections are either state parks or national forests. If your point of origin was Boston, that city has a wealth of historical and cultural attractions.

2

Arches National Park

Within this arid landscape is the world's greatest concentration of natural stone arches. There are approximately 90 of these formations that geologists consider true natural arches, including famous Landscape Arch, although more than 2,000 smaller ones have been catalogued. Landscape Arch is the world's longest such span at 306 feet. All are products of weathering and erosion, created over a period of several million years, in a process that continues to this day.

The landscape is quite harsh to the eye at first glance: hot and dry. Yet it is also a land of exquisite beauty, with the many arches, canyons, spires and balanced rock formations set against a brilliant blue sky. The primary colors are varying shades of reddish brown, especially photogenic in the early morning or late afternoon sunlight – and there is plenty of sunshine in this part of the country. It is appropriate that Arches is in a rather isolated part of the country, because the landscape evokes visions of another world from some science-fiction movie.

Facts & Figures

LOCATION/GATEWAYS/GETTING THERE: In southeastern Utah just five miles north of the town of Moab on US 191, the park is 30 miles south of I-70. There are no large cities nearby but a number of logical gateways present themselves. Las Vegas (via I-15 north to I-70 east) is almost 500 miles away. Yet, with the many attractions between these two points it is considered a convenient gateway to Arches. Salt Lake City is quite a bit closer (about 300 miles) via I-15 southbound to I-70 eastbound. Denver is approximately the same distance, via I-70 westbound, and can be an easy alternative gateway if you are going to combine some of the sights in Colorado with those in Utah.

YEAR ESTABLISHED: Previously a national monument, Arches became a national park in 1971.

SIZE: 73,379 acres (or 115 square miles).

ADMISSION FEE: $4 daily. The entrance permit is accepted at Canyonlands National Park as well.

CLIMATE/WHEN TO GO: Spring and fall are the best times to see the park as the weather is warm and bright. Winter isn't too cold to enjoy walking the trails either. The summer, on the other hand, is exceedingly hot, often over 100°F, and the sun can truly be relentless. If you do visit in the summer you should time your trip so that most of the touring can be completed in the morning hours before it really heats up. Carry water for yourself and your car and always wear a hat in the sun.

ADDRESS/TELEPHONE: Superintendent, Arches National Park, P.O. Box 907, Moab, UT 84532. (801) 259-8161.

Auto Tour/Short Stops

While a great many of the park's arches and other features are visible from the road or are just a short walk away, you might be disappointed with Arches if you don't hit the trail as well. But we'll begin with the suggested auto route, which covers about 55 miles of paved roadway. On this route you will see about a quarter of the approximately 90 major arch formations in the park.

Just inside the entrance to the park, after the road quickly winds its way up several hundred feet, is the visitor center. You should stop here to view the interesting exhibits explaining how Arches was formed. Here, too, is a short trail that will introduce you to the desert flora found in this region. A short distance past here is the southern terminus of the Park Avenue Trail. More will be said about this in the next section, but even if you don't walk down "Park Avenue," do at least get out to view it. The narrow, steeply rising rock formations are reminiscent of New York's Park Avenue

– a broad avenue flanked by columns of graceful skyscrapers. Among the best features of this area is the formation known as the **Three Gossips**. When viewed from the proper angle these giant stone monoliths appear to be three very tall women standing in a circle chatting about the neighbors (maybe their conversation is about visitors to the park who keep gawking at them!).

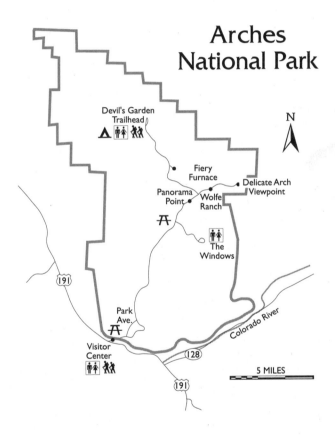

Over the next several miles the road passes the **Tower of Babel**, then an area called the **Rock Pinnacles**, before finally reaching the amazing **Balanced Rock**. It is difficult to understand how this huge boulder stays in place on its slim perch. A short trail circles the rock. Balanced Rock, besides being a unique attraction, is also a road junction, for here the road splits in two. Go first to the right, a spur road that is approximately five miles, round-trip. This leads to the **Windows Section** of the park. The name comes from the many small arches that look like the windows of a house when seen from a distance. While these can be seen from the road, you might want to take the trail here (see below).

Rejoining the main road, you then pass **Panorama Point**, with a view typical of the park's landscape, and then head down a recently paved road almost four miles to the **Delicate Arch Viewpoint**. As the name implies, this is one of the most graceful formations in the park. It can be clearly seen from an area reached by a short walk from the end of the road. You can get closer by traversing a difficult three-mile trail.

Return to the main road, turn right, and continue on, stopping to look at the surrounding canyon terrain, first at **Salt Valley Overlook** and, less than a mile later, **Fiery Furnace Viewpoint**. Shortly after passing **Skyline Arch**, you will come to the end of the road in the area known as the Devil's Garden. This is the trailhead for some major park landmarks that are described in the next section. After completing your visit here, turn around and drive the 20 miles back to the park's exit. This driving portion of the tour will take approximately three hours, including short walks.

Getting Out/Longer Stops

As mentioned previously, many of the park's most famous and beautiful sights cannot be readily seen from the road, so some trail activity is a must.

We previously cited **Park Avenue** as a worthy stop. Although you can get a good overview of the entire area from the roadside parking area and trailhead, it is an easy one-mile walk to the northern end. You will get a close-up view of features that could otherwise only be seen from a distance. This allows you to get a better feel for the park's formations (and their true size). Allow about 90 minutes for the round-trip. If one person in your party is willing to skip the walk, you can cut the time in half by having him or her take the car and meet you at the other end, so that the entire group doesn't have to backtrack.

To properly see the arches in the Windows Section you should take the mile-long loop trail that passes through the North and South Windows area. The route is sandy, as are most of the park's trails. On some of them you will sink into the sand up to your ankles, so dress appropriately. Despite these obstacles the trail can be completed in an hour or so and is well worth the time.

Landscape Arch, unfortunately, requires more effort to reach. It is a little over 1½ miles from the Devil's Garden parking area. The trail is hilly and a bit difficult. But if you take the 90-minute walk, you will be rewarded with a bird's-eye view of this magnificent arch, which dwarfs all others in the park. Several other arches are also visible from this trail. (The Devil's Garden Trail continues past Landscape Arch for several more miles.)

Accommodations & Dining

In keeping with Arches' primitive environment, there are no lodging or dining facilities in the park itself; however, the town of Moab is less than 10 minutes away and has a wide selection of places to stay and eat in all price ranges.

Where Do We Go From Here?

Arches National Park is best seen as a component of *Suggested Trip 7* in the last section of the book, since it is too far from any major city to be seen alone. On the bright side, **Canyonlands National Park** is only minutes away. One possible alternative to *Trip 7,* is to head south from Arches and see spectacular **Monument Valley** on the Arizona/Utah border.

3

Badlands National Park

Spanning 80 million years of geologic history, the biggest area of Badlands in the nation is an outstanding example of erosion and weathering. The fossil-rich area is both awe-inspiring in its beauty and, at the same time, dark and forbidding, despite traces of color in a mostly grayish-white and barren landscape. Deep ravines and jagged ridges dot the terrain. Although the land appears inhospitable, the Badlands provide a home to an unexpected diversity of animals and plants, and there is much to see in this unusual area Fortunately, despite the impression one might have, Badlands National Park is not difficult to see.

Facts & Figures

LOCATION/GATEWAYS/GETTING THERE: In the southwestern portion of South Dakota, east of the famous Black Hills region, Badlands National Park is accessible via the Badlands Loop Road (SR 240) from exits 110 (Wall) and 131 (Cactus Flat) of I-90. It is just over an hour's drive on the interstate from Rapid City, the nearest city with regular air service. Sioux Falls is about six hours east, also via I-90.

YEAR ESTABLISHED: First established as a national monument in 1929, the area was redesignated as a national park in 1978.

SIZE: 243,302 acres (or 380 square miles).

ADMISSION FEE: $5.

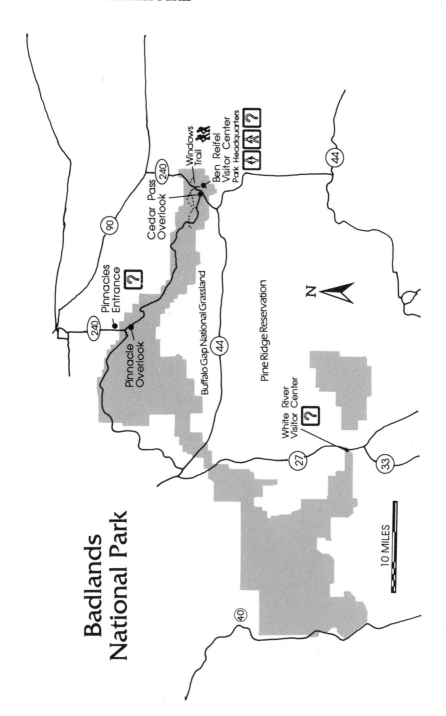

Badlands
National Park

Pinnacles
Entrance

Pinnacle
Overlook

240

240

90

Cedar Pass
Overlook

Windows
Trail

Ben Reifel
Visitor Center

Park Headquarters

44

Buffalo Gap National Grassland

44

Pine Ridge Reservation

N

White River
Visitor Center

27

33

40

10 MILES

CLIMATE/WHEN TO GO: The park is open all year, but winters are cold and there is a lot of snow. Summers tend to be hot but dry; hence, they are not so bad that they make a visit at this time unpleasant. There are frequent afternoon thunderstorms, some of which can be quite severe. Although summer is a good time to visit, if you can be here in fall or spring it is even better; the weather is very comfortable and the roads are not as crowded.

ADDRESS/TELEPHONE: Superintendent, Badlands National Park, P.O. Box 6, Interior, SD 57750. (605) 433-5361.

Auto Tour/Short Stops

Most of the park's major attractions and features are readily accessible via the Badlands Loop. This 27-mile-long road covers all but the park's isolated South Unit. You can choose either an east-west or west-east routing. For this discussion, we will assume that you'll begin from the Cactus Flat (or northeast) entrance of the park. The road through the central section of the park is winding and hilly, but not difficult to negotiate. Only in the beginning, where it rises from the relatively flat plain up to the rim drive, does it have steep grades and switchbacks. Each turn and dip brings with it new and exciting vistas. At the western end, the road drops back to the level of the surrounding area, but not as sharply as at the eastern end.

Along the Loop Road there are 13 overlooks, spaced more closely together in the generally more scenic eastern half of the park. You will want to stop at each one as they all provide clear views of typical Badland formations and they involve walking only a few feet from your car. In addition to these overlooks, there are some other attractions that you should not miss.

The **Cedar Pass Visitor Center**, reached after a thrilling drop in the road coming from the east, provides excellent information about the park's history and geology. A bit further on is the quarter-mile **Fossil Exhibit Trail**, containing replicas of fossil remains that have been found throughout the Badlands. It also has excellent views of distant Badland formations. Allow three hours for the Loop Road.

Getting Out/Longer Stops

Shortly after entering the eastern end of the park is the **Door Trail**, a popular and easy ¾-mile trail that leads to an opening in the rocky hill-like formation – hence the name. Through the "door" is a magnificent view of the Badlands, possibly the best in the entire park. Allow about 90 minutes.

The **Notch Trail** comes soon after the Door area. At 1½ miles, this trail is much more difficult. It involves climbing a ladder at one point, so be forewarned that it is not for everybody. It will take approximately two hours to complete.

Special Activities

Although the vast majority of visitors to the Badlands restrict themselves to the main Loop Road and its accompanying trails, the South Unit of the park also has some fantastic Badland formations. To reach the South Unit, exit from the Loop near its western terminus at Sage Creek. Follow this road to the small town of Scenic and then up to **Sheep Mountain Table** for an excellent overall panorama of the Badlands. It is the highest point in the park that is accessible by car. Note, however, that this graded road may be too difficult for drivers not accustomed to mountain driving and it may also be impassable in bad or wet weather no matter how much experience you have.

One additional item of interest, and one that all can partake of, is the prairie dog town in the extreme western portion of the park's main unit. If you are lucky you might just catch a glimpse of one of these shy creatures as they scamper to or from their underground homes.

Accommodations

There are three lodging facilities within the park itself, all in the vicinity of Cedar Pass. Although clean and comfortable, the **Badlands Inn** (24 motel rooms), **Badlands Motel** (six motel rooms) , and **Cedar Pass Lodge** (20 cabins) are very modest establishments (all B). Because of their small size it is important to make reservations far in advance. Right outside the park is a 10-room **Budget Host Motel** (B). Since you will probably not need to extend your visit here over two days (unless you are doing the North Trail and the South Unit), you may be more comfortable staying in Wall, which offers a much greater variety of lodgings.

Dining

The **Cedar Pass Lodge** is the only place in the park with a restaurant. However, a good variety of restaurants can be found in Wall, including the world famous **Wall Drug**.

Where Do We Go From Here?

Trip 2 in the last section of the book incorporates the Badlands National Park. If you are unable to do that entire trip, the proximity of the park to the beautiful **Black Hills** (including Mount Rushmore) makes a good, relatively short trip. If you do not like the available airline connections into Rapid City, then your trip will involve much more driving, either from Sioux Falls or Denver, but then there are more sightseeing possibilities available to you.

4

Big Bend National Park

Encompassing a vast tract of wilderness on the north side of a very "big bend" in the Rio Grande River bordering Mexico, the park combines both desert and mountain terrain. It also contains many striking geologic structures, notably the several deep, sharp-walled canyons.

Because of variations in elevations from less than 3,000 to almost 8,000 feet, Big Bend, although in desert country, has many different climatic zones, which produce a wide variety of wildlife and vegetation. The latter is of special interest. The many barren and rocky areas are a sharp contrast to both the desert flowers and cactus that blooms a brilliant white and the heavily forested mountain slopes just a few miles away.

There is a little of everything at Big Bend, but you'll probably be most impressed by the beauty of the rugged Chisos Mountains and their precipitous canyons.

Facts & Figures

LOCATION/GATEWAYS/GETTING THERE: This may be the least accessible of the parks in this volume. Big Bend is about 300 miles from El Paso via I-10, US 90 and SR 118. From the east, it can be reached from San Antonio via US 90 and US 385, a distance of about 360 miles. The park is tucked into a small corner of southwestern Texas.

YEAR ESTABLISHED: The park was established in 1935 and remains one of the lesser-known major units of the National Park System.

SIZE: 741,118 acres (or 1,158 square miles), an area just about the same size as the state of Rhode Island.

ADMISSION FEE: $5.

CLIMATE/WHEN TO GO: The weather varies widely from the desert areas to the mountain heights and back to the canyons. There is also great variation within a single day in many sections. It is not advisable to visit in the heat of the summer, because daytime temperatures, although relatively comfortable in the mountains, can be well over 100°F in the lower desert areas. Probably the best time to visit is between March and May. Not only is the temperature more comfortable, but this is also the time (especially during the early part of the period) when the desert cactus is in bloom and there are beautiful white flowers almost everywhere you look.

ADDRESS/TELEPHONE: Superintendent, Big Bend National Park, TX 79834. (915) 477-2251.

Auto Tour/Short Stops

Your visit to Big Bend National Park will be in the form of a long loop from either Alpine (via SR 118) or Marathon (via US 385). From one point to the other, it is a circuit of 187 miles, of which not quite one-fifth is within the park itself. This does not include close to another 100 miles of side roads leading to the park's main features along the Rio Grande. It does not matter from which end you begin, but we will work our way through the park from the SR 118 entrance.

As you pass by the Maverick Ranger Station at the park's entrance, the road starts to climb dramatically with views of Tule Mountain on your right and, a bit later, Croton Peak to your left. Approximately 10 miles into the park, turn off the main route and follow the side road to its end, about 25 miles distant. En route are mountain views and the canyon of the Blue Creek. View stops should be made at the **Sotol Vista**, **Burro Mesa Pouroff** and **Mule Ears** overlooks, most of which are on very short spurs from the canyon road. Along the last eight miles the road parallels the majestic **Santa Elena Canyon**. There are several vantage points from which you can walk to the rim and see the Rio Grande, more than 1,000 feet below. The opposite rim is in Mexico.

Then reverse your route back to the main park road as it continues to wind its way alongside mountain peaks. In about 12 miles another turnoff leads six miles down a spur route to the Basin campground area and a ranger information station. From here there are excellent views of 7,835-foot **Emory Peak**, highest in the park, and 7,535-foot **Lost Mine Peak**. (Several trails are here; see the following section.)

Rejoining the main road once again you will soon come to Panther Junction and the park headquarters area. Here you can get information and see exhibits on the park. Then, at the junction, take the side road to **Boquillas Canyon**. This trip is over 35 miles and very near the end it divides into two short spurs that lead to observation points with excellent canyon vistas. Boquillas Canyon is quite different from Santa Elena, as the Rio Grande in this area has significantly more turns. Also, the angle of the sun will have changed, leading to a completely different perspective.

Return to the main park route where the road will now begin to drop, but not nearly as steeply at the very beginning of the journey. You will shortly reach a roadside exhibit area of fossilized bones, all of which were found within the park. Continuing on, the park ends at Persimmon Gap. You will have covered a lot of miles and many beautiful sights on the Auto Tour, so allow between six and seven hours to complete it all.

Getting Out/Longer Stops

Besides brief walks along the two main canyons, there is a picturesque nature trail leading to Lost Mine Peak. The way is not particularly difficult, but it is long, requiring three hours for the round-trip – of course you can opt to do only part of it if that's too long. Shorter, more strenuous walks lead to formations known as the South Rim and the Window, but they require 1 to 1½ hours apiece. The canyon bottoms are also accessible by trail, but these are extremely difficult and should NOT be attempted by anyone without experience in such activities, especially in hot weather.

Big Bend National Park

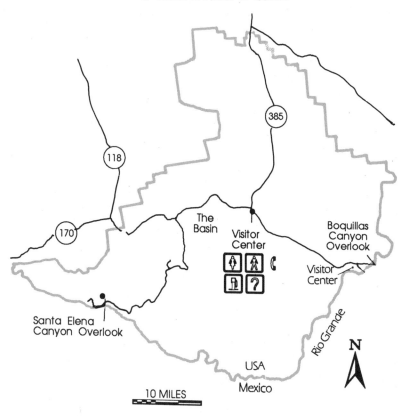

Special Activities

For the more adventurous visitor there are **horseback trips** into the park interior lasting from 2½ hours to a full day. There also multiple-day **river trips**, though some involve intense white water and are definitely not for beginners ($).

Accommodations

Chisos Mountain Lodge (with 34 motel-type rooms) is the only place to stay inside the park. It is located in the Basin area and provides decent accommodations (M). You should make reservations well in advance, preferably six or more months ahead of time, and plan your trip so that you will be around the Basin at the end of the day to avoid many miles of extra driving. Both Alpine and Marathon have hotels, but they are not especially close to the park. Depending upon your arrival and departure times, you may find that staying there is convenient. In-park lodging reservations are through National Parks Concessions Inc., (915) 477-2291.

Dining

The **Chisos Mountain Lodge** has both a full-service restaurant and a coffee shop. More extensive choices are also to be found in Alpine and Marathon.

Where Do We Go From Here?

Trip 4 from El Paso includes Big Bend on its list of attractions. Should you be coming from the east (i.e., the more populated portion of Texas), there aren't many scenic attractions in that part of the state but you can see its many historic points of interest and its impressive cities. San Antonio, with the Alamo and the Paseo del Rio, is the nearest city other than El Paso.

5

Black Canyon of the Gunnison National Monument

Incorporating 12 miles along the deepest portion of the Gunnison River gorge, this is one of the most amazing sights in the country. Although there are other canyons that may be deeper, longer, or even a bit narrower, there is no other that combines so many extraordinary features in such a small area.

The product of more than two million years of cutting action by the river, the canyon reaches a maximum depth of almost 2,700 feet below the rim. In some places at the top it is as little as 1,200 feet from one rim to the other – it seems you can almost reach out and touch the opposite side. At one point on the bottom the canyon narrows to only 40 feet! In fact, there are only a few places where the width exceeds the depth, which is unusual for a canyon. But, then again, the Black Canyon is not an ordinary canyon. The name comes from two factors: much of the canyon is in shadow because sunlight cannot penetrate its narrow opening; secondly, the rock itself is a dark color. Its walls really are sheer drops. Two of the most spectacular are **Painted Wall** and **Chasm Wall** which drop, respectively, 2,250 and 1,180 feet. Black Canyon may not be well known but, once seen, it will leave a lasting impression.

Facts & Figures

LOCATION/GATEWAYS/GETTING THERE: The monument is just off US 50 east of the town of Montrose in west-central Colorado. It is 65 miles from the Grand Junction exit of I-70 and about 250 miles from Denver via US 50 and US 285. Allow six hours for the latter drive. This description applies to the South Rim; see the North Rim section at the end of this chapter.

YEAR ESTABLISHED: The Black Canyon of the Gunnison became a national monument in 1933.

SIZE: 20,763 acres (or 32 square miles).

ADMISSION FEE: $4.

CLIMATE/WHEN TO GO: The South Rim is open all year, but only the beginning of the road may be open when there has been heavy snow. The main travel season is May through October. Summers are quite warm but usually not uncomfortable.

ADDRESS/TELEPHONE: Superintendent, Black Canyon of the Gunnison National Monument, 2233 East Main, Montrose, CO 81402. (303) 249-7036.

Auto Tour/Short Stops

The South Rim road extends three miles from its beginning at the monument entrance to the end of the line and it provides easy access via short trails to several overlooks with spectacular views. The contrast between the often sun-drenched overlook areas and the dark, gloomy recesses of the canyon's interior are as staggering as the immensity of the sheer canyon walls. As the road is short, you should plan to stop at all of the overlooks; but the very best views are at **Gunnison Point, Chasm View, Sunset View** and **High Point**. If you look east or west instead of across at the North Rim you will see the length of the canyon between the great walls of the gorge and more fully appreciate just how narrow it is.

It will take a little more than an hour to see the monument's South Rim, including a stop at the visitor center at the monument entrance.

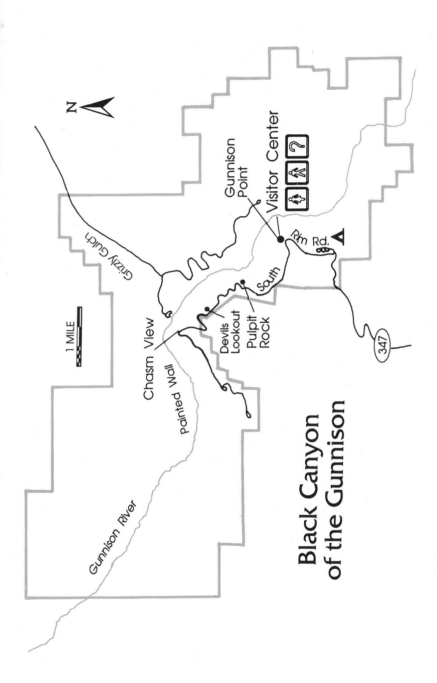

Getting Out/Longer Stops

Although descents are allowed into the canyon (upon notification of a Park Ranger), all such trips are arduous and should not be attempted by the casual visitor. As the monument is relatively small and confined to the canyon rim, there are no long hikes that can be suggested. You can, however, walk along portions of the rim instead of riding from one overlook to the next. There is only one long trail leading to the rim – the 1½-mile **Warren Point Trail** at road's end.

The North Rim

Although it provides vistas just as fantastic as those from the South Rim, the North Rim is much harder to reach. It is accessible only by a 14-mile graded road, the last two miles of which are along the canyon's rim. It is only open from May to October and there are no visitor facilities. If you are interested, you can get there via SR 92 from either Delta (between Grand Junction and Montrose if coming from the west) or from just past the town of Sapinero in the Curecanti Recreation Area if coming from the east. The spur road leaves SR 92 at Crawford. Additional mileage from the entrance road on the South Rim to the North Rim is about 75 miles one way, regardless of which route you take.

Accommodations & Dining

There is no overnight lodging within the monument nor is food available. However, there is a good choice of both in the nearby town of Montrose. There are more facilities 57 miles east on US 50 in the town of Gunnison, just past the Curecanti National Recreation Area.

Where Do We Go From Here?

Suggested Trip 3 is a scenic loop through Colorado and includes the Black Canyon. It is an ideal excursion for those seeking spectacular scenery, but it can also be condensed if you want to see the Black Canyon on a shorter trip.

6

Bryce Canyon National Park

Although young in geological terms compared to some of its equally famous neighbors, Bryce Canyon is one of the most remarkable examples of nature in the world. It is one of the main reasons why this section of the country – southern Utah – is called "Color Country," a region blessed with an abundance of such wonders. This land of unusually shaped pinnacles, spires, and arches come in a staggering array of colors, including pink, red, and rust. Patches of green (which are actually the tops of trees in the canyon) also dot the landscape. The shapes are a result of erosion; the colors come from a combination of mineral deposits in the stone and the play of sunlight. According to geologists, the park is not a canyon at all, despite it's name. It is, rather, a series of amphitheaters in the shape of a horseshoe. The name given to it by native Indians translates roughly as "Red rocks standing like men in a bowl-shaped canyon." Indeed, no words in the English language could describe it more succinctly than that.

A government surveyor in 1876 said of Bryce that it is the "wildest and most wonderful scene that the eye of man ever beheld." In reality, Bryce is a land where seeing is not believing. It is not uncommon for visitors to stand and stare at a particular view or formation as if in a trance, then come back and look again. Travelers who have been to many of our national parks usually rank Bryce high on their list of favorites.

Facts & Figures

LOCATION/GATEWAYS/GETTING THERE: In the southwestern portion of Utah, Bryce is reached from I-15 via SR 14, US 89 and SR 12 from Cedar City from the south. From the north, exit at I-15 via SR 20 and take that to US 89, then SR 12. It is about a 4½-hour drive from Las Vegas, or 5½ to 6 hours if coming from Salt Lake City. Those are the nearest commercial airports that you can reach easily. Either way the roads are excellent and the scenery during the second half of the journey is superb – so much so that you won't mind how long it takes to get there.

YEAR ESTABLISHED: Mormon settlers were the first white men in this area, one of whom the park is named after. It was surveyed in the 1870s, and was given the status of a national park in 1924.

SIZE: 36,010 acres (or 56 square miles). It is not one of the biggest of our national parks but, acre for acre, it packs a wallop that can hardly be equaled.

ADMISSION FEE: $5.

CLIMATE/WHEN TO GO: Although beautiful in wintertime when it is snow-covered, the first-time visitor should see it without a blanket of white. Because of the high elevation (most of the canyon rim is 8-9,000 feet above sea level), the summer is quite pleasant. The main touring season, when most facilities are open, is from May 1st through the end of October. Brief afternoon thunderstorms in summer provide most of the rain in this generally arid area. Be advised that during these storms lightning frequently strikes the rim; so be prepared to seek shelter when the skies open up.

ADDRESS/TELEPHONE: Superintendent, Bryce Canyon National Park, Bryce Canyon, UT 84717. (801) 834-5322.

Auto Tour/Short Stops

As a casual visitor, you can see Bryce Canyon quite easily from your car and with relatively short, easy walks. The main road extends from the park entrance almost directly south to Rainbow Point, a distance of just over 20 miles. The road comes to a dead end so that the round-trip, including allowance for a few short spur roads, is under 50 miles.

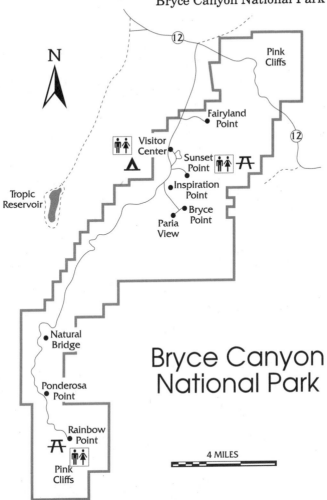

N

Pink
Cliffs

Fairyland
Point

Visitor
Center

Sunset
Point

Tropic
Reservoir

Inspiration
Point

Bryce
Point

Paria
View

Natural
Bridge

Bryce Canyon
National Park

Ponderosa
Point

Rainbow
Point

4 MILES

Pink
Cliffs

Although relatively small, the park contains an enormous amount to see, including views from 13 roadside overlooks. Two possible methods of touring Bryce are to drive all the way to the end and use the return trip to make your view stops, or to see everything on the way down. An even better approach is to plan your trip so that there are stops in both directions. This has the advantage of letting you see some of the best features at different times, so that the sunlight will probably make you wonder if you had previously been at that spot at all. This narrative will describe all attractions from north to south (that is, from the park entrance to the end of the road).

Almost immediately after you pass through the entrance station, watch carefully for a spur road on your left that leads to **Fairyland**

View. The name tells all. While this view is certainly not atypical of what you will see throughout Bryce, if it is your first stop on the rim it may well be the most dramatic. Here, like all the other stops on the Auto Tour, the canyon rim overlooks are just a few yards from the parking areas.

Rejoining the main road, in less than a mile you will reach the **Bryce Canyon Visitor Center**, where there are excellent exhibits on the geological history of the park and information on activities. All trailers must be unhitched and remain here since they are not permitted south of the visitor center. A loop road leaves the main road and gets closer to the canyon edge, providing excellent access to two brilliant vistas: **Sunrise Point** and **Sunset Point**. It is just as awesome, perhaps more so, to stand on the rim between these two points and see both at once (see next section for details). The two points face each other around the largest of the natural amphitheaters that comprise Bryce. This one is two miles wide, three miles long and reaches depths of nearly 600 feet. The short loop road will then meet up with the main road; very soon thereafter you will be at **Inspiration Point**, one of the park's outstanding and most popular views.

From here there is a T-shaped spur leading to two other majestic overlooks by the names of **Bryce Point** and **Paria View**. After you return to the main road, it will be about 10 miles to your next stop. The scenery during this interval will remain highly pleasing. Besides more distant views of the colorful, soldier-like spires, this portion of the road passes through terrain that is partially forested. The elevation in the southern half of the park is higher and it is during this part of your journey that the road rises in a series of gentle switchbacks and turns. You are more likely to see wildlife during this time than at any other point on the rim.

Now you will have reached **Farview Point**, and soon after that is **Natural Bridge**, the largest such structure in the park and one of the more famous formations in Bryce. From many of the frequent overlooks in this area you will be able to see other natural bridges and several arches as well as the much more common pinnacles and spires. **Yovimpo Point** is the next view stop and it comes just before the end of the road at **Rainbow Point**. Looking north from this last viewpoint you will see an amazing panorama of rock-filled amphitheaters, many of which you passed on the way down (or actually, up) and looking quite different from this vantage point. At 9,102 feet, Rainbow Point is the highest elevation of any viewpoint on the Canyon Rim Road.

You will certainly regret that the road goes no farther, but the consolation is that you can, if you wish, do it all over again on the way back! And that is one of the greatest pleasures of Bryce – because even a small change in the angle of sunlight (or the angle at which you view it) has an enormous effect on the coloring in the canyon; the same spot will look very different if seen even a short time later or earlier. It makes for endless variety – truly a sightseeing bonanza.

Including driving time and stops at the visitor center and the observation points suggested, it should take you less than four hours to complete the Auto Tour of Bryce Canyon.

Getting Out/Longer Stops

Although the high elevation helps keep summers cool, it can also make even relatively short walks a bit tiring for some, so do consider this before attempting anything in this section, especially trails involving descents below the canyon rim. Although the latter are difficult, everyone who has walked along even a small portion of the 22-mile **Under the Rim Trail** can enthusiastically report that the views of the imaginatively-named formations are a worthy reward for the effort. (When you are on the rim's edge you will frequently see people moving about in the narrow, tunnel-like passages beneath the rim. Do not throw anything in as you may injure to hikers.)

An easy but still exhilarating walk is between the overlooks at Sunrise and Sunset Points. The distance between the two is less than three-quarters of a mile (round-trip of 1½ miles). The trail is quite level and you will get views of the canyon that are generally not available from the overlooks alone. Allow more than an hour for this walk, or half that time if one member of your party skips the walk and meets the rest of you with the car at the other end. This trail is actually a portion of the 5½-mile **Rim Trail**, which extends all the way from Fairyland to Bryce Point. You can access this trail at many points along the rim drive, making it possible to view the canyon in a great number of places through a series of short walks. The trail is almost always level. While there are railings at the overlooks by most parking areas, the Rim Trail itself has no such protective barriers, and the trail is right at the edge. It presents no danger so long as you don't do anything foolhardy, but parents should keep a very close watch over small children.

The **Navajo Loop, Fairyland** and **Tower Bridge Trails** all descend into the canyon. While going down may seem easy enough, remember that the return trip involves an ascent ranging up to 750 feet, making these trails of 1½ to eight miles trails very strenuous. Time required varies from about two hours for the shortest (the Navajo Loop) to five hours or more for the longest. Be sure to carry plenty of drinking water. The Navajo Loop descends a bit over 500 feet. Among the formations you will pass on the trail: Wall Street, the Camel and Wise Man, and Thor's Hammer.

For those of you who want to go into the canyon without the exertion required on the aforementioned trails, the **Queens Garden Trail** at Sunrise Point is the easiest below-the-rim excursion. The 1½-mile, two-hour hike visits one of the park's most scenic areas. The return climb of 320 feet can be handled by most people – just take it slow. All in all, a below-rim walk will be a worthwhile part of any visit to Bryce.

Special Activities

If you are not up to the rigors of exploring the canyon on foot, consider a **horseback ride** instead ($). Be aware that, although not as hard on your legs, this too can be strenuous. Inquire at the visitor center. **Helicopter flights** are available from private operators just north of the park entrance ($).

Accommodations

Bryce Canyon Lodge, near the visitor center, is an attractive and historic log structure with 110 units, 40 of which are rustic cabins (E). One of the nice things about staying here is that you are less than a five-minute walk from the rim, so you can gaze out upon the canyon whenever you get the urge. For reservations, contact TW Recreational Services at (801) 586-7688.

Another establishment is actually one mile north of the park, but special mention is warranted for the 117-room **Best Western Ruby's Inn.** This motor inn has excellent facilities, including a general store that has everything from mementos of your trip to personal needs to one-hour film developing. It is my first choice (M).

Dining

The formal restaurant at the **Bryce Canyon Lodge** is very good, as are the two restaurants at **Ruby's Inn**.

Where Do We Go From Here?

Bryce Canyon can be seen in conjunction with the itinerary of *Suggested Trip 7*. However, it is also a very common practice to see Bryce, **Zion National Park** and the North Rim of the **Grand Canyon** in a shorter loop trip from Las Vegas. These three attractions can also be visited from Salt Lake City, but the mileage is much greater.

Not far from Bryce is a miniature version of what you have just seen, called **Cedar Breaks National Monument**. If your route to or from Bryce passes through Cedar City, then you should definitely include it on your schedule. Even better, organize your trip so that you see Cedar Breaks on your way to Bryce – it's an excellent appetizer!

7

Canyonlands & Capitol Reef

Before getting started let me caution you that these two parks are not adjacent to one another. In fact, they are separated by a drive that will take the better part of a day. Canyonlands is much closer both geographically and in geological terms to Arches National Park than it is to Capitol Reef. So why, then, are they together here? Well, compared to virtually every other park, monument or recreation area in this book, these two are quite primitive. Facilities for visitors are limited and there are fewer paved roads extending into the two parks' interiors than in most other parks described in this book. But a trip to either of them will provide you with an experience that can only be classified as spectacular. Canyonlands, as the name implies, is an area of deep, awesome canyons. But it is much more than that. It is a land filled with arches, spires and mesas of all shapes and sizes, a fantasy land where nature has gone wild.

At Capitol Reef, the dominating landscape is a wall-like cliff, nearly a thousand feet high, that runs like an ocean reef for a distance of 90 miles. The tops of these cliffs are a white sandstone that many people say resembles the United States Capitol – hence the name. This "Land of the Sleeping Rainbow," as the Navajo called it, is also a place of many beautiful hues.

Facts & Figures

LOCATION/GATEWAYS/GETTING THERE: Both parks are located in the southern portion of Utah known as Color Country; Capitol Reef is in the central portion, while Canyonlands is in the eastern part right near Arches National Park. If coming from Las Vegas, access to these parks is best described in the itinerary of *Trip 7*. From Salt Lake City, take I-15 south to US 50 at the town of Scipio. Near Salina pick up SR 24 if going to Capitol Reef first, otherwise take I-70 from Salina east to US 191, then head south to the Canyonlands. It is five hours from Salt Lake City to Capitol Reef and about 6½ hours to Canyonlands.

There are only two routes to get from part of the park to the other. From Canyonlands to Capitol Reef the shorter route is via the town of Green River. Take US 191 north to I-70, then head west to SR 24, with that road taking you directly to Capitol Reef. This is a 4½-hour, 160-mile scenic drive. The other way is via Blanding. Head south on US 191 to SR 95, staying on 95 until reaching SR 24 and then on to the park. This is a 6½-hour journey covering almost 270 miles. There are more sights en route if you go this way. As a matter of fact, if you follow *Trip 7* you will be covering both of these routes on your circuit through wonderful Color Country.

YEAR ESTABLISHED: Canyonlands was the first of the two to be made a national park, in 1964. Capitol Reef joined the club in 1971.

SIZE: Canyonlands – 337,570 acres (or 527 square miles). Capitol Reef – 241,904 acres (or 378 square miles).

ADMISSION FEES: Canyonlands – $5 (reciprocal privileges given at Arches National Park). Capitol Reef – $3.

CLIMATE/WHEN TO GO: Both are in arid country, with strong sun-filled days characterizing the blazing hot summers (this is especially so in Canyonlands). Winters are chilly and snow is not unknown. Overall, the best time to visit is in late spring or early fall.

ADDRESS/TELEPHONE: Canyonlands – Superintendent, Canyonlands National Park, 125 W. 200 South, Moab, UT 84532. (801) 259-7164. Capitol Reef – Superintendent, Capitol Reef National Park, Torrey, UT 84795. (801) 425-3791.

Canyonlands
National Park

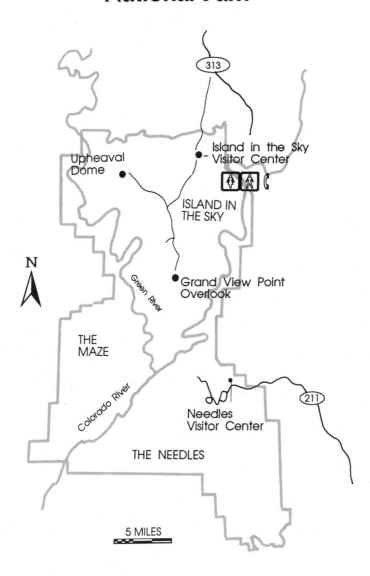

Canyonlands National Park

Auto Tour/Getting Out

We'll combine these two headings because most of the trails are of a back-country nature; even the relatively short ones are rather difficult. A major reconstruction of the road system in Canyonlands, which started in the mid 1980s, has recently been completed. The original road network consisted solely of unpaved and difficult roads. Over 20 miles of this system are now nicely paved, making driving much easier. Unfortunately, at this time, the modernization does not include the building of new roads into the interior, so most of the park is still inaccessible to cars. This also applies to most visitor facilities. Check on the status of road closings before travelling on any of the unpaved roads.

The confluence of the Colorado and Green Rivers divides the park into three distinct sections, as well as creating the roaring river rapids that form spectacular **Cataract Canyon**, the many twisting bends of **Meander Canyon**, and the comparatively tranquil **Stillwater Canyon**. The three sections are Islands in the Sky, where most of your visit will be concentrated, the Needles, and the Maze, the last of which is not on our tour at all because it is considered to be one of the most inaccessible portions of all the national parks in America.

As you enter the park via SR 313, you'll reach the **Island in The Sky Visitor Center**. Stop here to view the exhibits on Canyonlands and ask any questions you may have about your visit. Just south of the center is an overlook where you can peer down into **Shaefer Canyon**. (A rough side road leads down into the canyon.) About four miles further along the route, the road splits. First, head toward the right, stopping at the **Holeman Springs Canyon Overlook** before reaching the end of the road at White Rock. From here, a relatively short trail leads to one of the park's outstanding features, **Upheaval Dome**, whose origin scientists continue to argue about. Retrace your route towards the split, first going down a short unpaved spur where a fantastic view awaits at the **Green River Overlook**. Now head down the road, stopping for the views at **Candlestick Tower Overlook** and **Buck Canyon Overlook**. At the end of the road, just beyond the very colorful **Orange Cliffs Overlook** is the parking area for the **Grand View Point Overlook**. This is a place of unbelievable beauty perched high above the river valleys and from here you'll get a fantastic overall picture of the park's many geological wonders.

The **Needles** section is on the other side of the Colorado River, but the park roads don't connect the two areas. You have to exit the park and follow SR 313 back to US 191 south, a total distance of 39 miles, to the junction of SR 211. Then head west on this road for another 48 miles. The road will re-enter the park and traverse the thousands of rock spires that give this section of the park its name. The viewpoint at the end of the paved road is one of the very best in the entire park. Several other pull-outs are dotted along the route. Then reverse your route. It should be pointed out that all of the mileage is not really extra if you are going to be taking (or are coming from) the Blanding route to Capitol Reef, because you would have to go this way in any event. If you are not going to visit Capitol Reef, you might think twice before undertaking the extra mileage to get to the Needles section.

The time needed to see Canyonlands (from entering the Islands in the Sky section to exiting from the Needles), a total of about 160 miles, is a minimum of seven hours.

Special Activities

If this wonderful scenery has whetted your appetite and you feel frustrated that you can't get to see more, there are a number of **jeep tours** into the park's interior. Most of these leave from the town of Moab; some depart from Monticello ($). Inquire locally for prices and schedules.

Accommodations & Dining

There are no facilities inside the park. The town of Moab, however, is less than an hour away and has a wide choice of facilities.

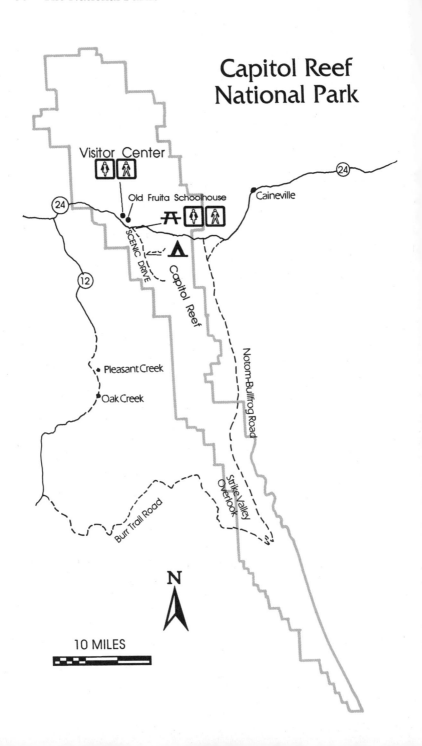

Capitol Reef
National Park

N

10 MILES

Capitol Reef National Park

Auto Tour/Getting Out

Recent improvements at Capitol Reef make it easier to visit than in the past, but most of the trails are still long and very strenuous, so we'll combine the Auto Tour and Getting Out sections once again. Along SR 24, which runs west-east through the park, are a number of interesting stops. The first is **Panorama Viewpoint**. Even better views are available if you take the unpaved spur road from Panorama about a half a mile to the end. From there, two short trails (each less than a mile round-trip) lead to the **Goosenecks Overlook** and **Sunset Point**, where the lighting at day's end is no less than spectacular. Other points of interest on SR 24 are the **Twin Rocks**, **Chimney Rock**, **The Castle** and **Capitol Dome**, a massive rock formation that is one of the park's most famous sights. The **Fruita Visitor Center** is also on this road.

Leading off SR 24 is the seven-mile **Scenic Drive**, which heads south into the park's heartland along a geologic formation known as the **Water Pocket Fold**. It is this formation which gives the "Reef" part of the name to this area. The drive is easy and the view of the multi-colored wall of rock is impressive. Unfortunately, here's where the trails are longer and more difficult. The best ones are reached, if you're interested, via unpaved spur roads at Grand Wash and Capitol Gorge. Allow a total of 2-2½ hours for visiting Capitol Reef.

Special Activities

A good way to add fun to your visit during the summer is to **pick fruit** that grows in the Fruita area (near the visitor center). From June through October you'll find (depending upon which month you visit) cherries, apricots, peaches, pears and apples. There's no charge as long as you consume the fruit within the park. Fees apply if you take quantities of fruit out of the park.

Accommodations & Dining

Facilities for spending the night and eating are very limited in this area. There are absolutely none in the park. The nearest options are a few miles west of the park in the town of Bicknell. More modest accommodations are available in Torrey or east of the park in Hanksville.

Where Do We Go From Here?

(Applies to both parks). If you look carefully at a map of Utah you will see that these parks form a vital and convenient link to the many attractions suggested in *Trip 7*. I strongly advise that you follow that itinerary. Any trip that includes Arches, Bryce Canyon, Zion, these two parks and other scenic highlights of Color Country is worth just about any amount of time and effort to see.

8

Carlsbad Caverns National Park

Although Carlsbad Caverns does not quite have the same extensive network of passageways and sub-caverns found in Mammoth Cave, it is justly noted for having chambers of enormous size and unusual beauty. Still, too, its 21 miles of known caverns make it one of the largest in the world.

The natural entrance is through a massive archway that reaches 90 feet across and 40 feet high at its greatest point. Inside, you will enter another world; a world of beautiful and sometimes delicate structures. Often, these formations are surprisingly alive with color. Some 200 million years of earth's history are contained within the cavern.

But some people who visit put the wonders of the cave itself in a position of only secondary importance. They come to visit the cave's famous residents – a huge population of bats. These strange creatures emerge from the cave on summer evenings in a spectacular and unusual display that is really quite beyond the ability of words to describe. We will, however, do our best to cover it as well as the cave itself, a combination that makes Carlsbad Caverns a unique destination.

Facts & Figures

LOCATION/GATEWAYS/GETTING THERE: At the town of Whites City in the southeastern portion of New Mexico not far from the Texas state line, Carlsbad Caverns is reached via US 180, a 160- mile, three-hour trip from El Paso. It can also be reached via I-40, US 285 and US 180 from Albuquerque. This is about a six-hour trip.

YEAR ESTABLISHED: The caverns were made a national monument in 1923 and received a promotion to national park just seven years later in 1930.

SIZE: 46,755 acres (or 73 square miles).

ADMISSION FEE: Entrance to the park is free. Cave tours vary in price beginning at $5 and dependent upon length and nature of the tour.

CLIMATE/WHEN TO GO: This desert country has mild winters and very hot summer days. Evenings are more pleasant. However, since the majority of your activities are "inside," the surface weather conditions are not that important. The cave is always 56°F, a temperature that makes a sweater or light jacket appropriate at all times. Your visit should be made between May and October when the bats make their appearance. To visit at any other time would be to miss half the story.

ADDRESS/TELEPHONE: Superintendent, Carlsbad Caverns National Park, 3225 National Parks Highway, Carlsbad, NM 88220. (505) 785-2232.

Auto Tour/Getting Out

As was mentioned earlier, this park is an underground experience and outdoor walks and vistas from your car are not what most visitors are looking for or expecting.

However, the seven-mile drive from the entrance to the visitor center rises dramatically through a dark canyon. Other good views can be seen from the one-way, 10-mile **Walnut Canyon Desert Drive**. It is a gravel road, but well maintained. At the visitor center itself you'll find excellent displays on the park's natural and human history as well as that of the surrounding area. Access to back-country trails are on the Walnut Canyon Drive and on the road to Slaughter Canyon Cave (via County Route 418). These trails are all long, difficult and primitive. For most of you, the cave and the bats is what it's all about, so we'll move on to that right now.

Carlsbad Caverns National Park

To Carlsbad

Walnut Canyon Desert Drive

Visitor Center

White's City

Rattlesnake Canyon Trail

GUADALUPE MOUNTAINS

North Slaughter Canyon Trail

Slaughter Canyon

Rattlesnake Springs

Yucca Canyon Trail

180

418

62

N

5 MILES

Special Activities

The main cave can be visited on one or more of three different tours. These are called the Natural Entrance Route, the Big Room Route, and the Kings Palace Guided Tour. Access to both the Big Room and the Kings Palace is via an elevator. The first route follows a twisting one-mile course and is moderately difficult to strenuous. This tour has no facilities for handicapped individuals. The Big Room Route is also about a mile, but is relatively flat and even has sections that are handicapped-accessible. Finally, the Kings Palace Guided Tour is easier than the Natural Entrance Route but more difficult than the Big Room. It lasts about 1¼ hours. You should allow at least an hour for the Big Room and about 90 minutes for the Natural Entrance Route.

NATURAL ENTRANCE ROUTE: You enter through the natural archway and take a twisting, dizzying drop through the Main Corridor, descending a total of 830 feet to the **Green Lake Room**, so-called because of a small pond there. Then you go into the **King's Chamber**, a large and almost circular room, followed immediately by the **Queen's Chamber**. Here the fantastic formations are mainly in the form of "elephant ears" or "draperies." The room is also known for its delicate pink and rose colored hues when illuminated. Now you move on to the **Papoose Room** and then to the cavern lunchroom (reasonably priced snacks and lunches are available).

BIG ROOM ROUTE: Leaving the elevator, you enter the immense **Big Room**, cross-shaped and measuring 1,800 by 1,100 feet at one point. As if those dimensions aren't impressive enough, the ceiling reaches the staggering maximum height of 255 feet – it could accommodate a 25-story skyscraper! The room contains many odd formations that are reminiscent of such things as totem poles. You exit the cave by elevator.

KINGS PALACE GUIDED TOUR: This used to be part of the self-guiding Big Room Tour, but was changed to a guided tour only because careless or mischievous visitors were breaking delicate formations in this part of the cave. On this tour you'll explore four "rooms" containing some of the most beautiful formations in the entire cave.

Plan on touring the caves early in the day, since the final trips depart about 4:30 in the summer and earlier during the off-season. Sign up for the guided tour at the visitor center. We suggest that you, at a minimum, do the Big Room and Kings Palace routes and highly recommend the Natural Entrance Route as long as you're physically able to do so.

And now... about those bats. Forget everything you think you know about these harmless, useful, and certainly misunderstood animals. The cave is home to about 14 species of bats, the majority of which are Mexican freetails – no vampire bats here (and they don't deserve their reputation either). Every night from May to October, people gather in the amphitheater outside the cave. At sundown a park ranger gives an interesting talk about the bats and what you are going to see. At dusk the spectacle begins. All is quiet; soon you will begin to hear the fluttering of wings as the first bats emerge from the cave. At first there are only a few, but then they come out at the rate of up to 300 per second, filling the sky completely with their black silhouettes. Some come so close to the crowd that you can actually feel a breeze from their wings. (Don't worry, they won't get in your hair, but some people will let out a shriek. It's all part of the fun.) In all, a million or more bats may emerge in a procession that can last as long as an hour, especially during the height of the season in August and September. They will return at dawn after an evening of dining on insects. The sight is sure to be remembered. Of course, the portion of the cave where the bats reside during the day is off limits to all visitors.

Note on Slaughter Canyon

Slaughter Canyon Cave is a separate cave within Carlsbad Caverns National Park, and is a 40-minute drive from the visitor center. Although you don't have to be a spelunker to visit Slaughter Canyon, it is quite a bit more difficult than the other caves in this book. You have to carry your own flashlight and water supply and the trip is quite strenuous. I wouldn't recommend it for the first-time visitor to Carlsbad.

Accommodations & Dining

There is no lodging within the park (unless you are a bat), but there is a motel near the park entrance at Whites City, with a far bigger selection in nearby Carlsbad. Food service within the park is limited to the lunchroom that is visited as part of the cave tours.

Where Do We Go From Here?

Trip 4 includes Carlsbad and is the logical extension since there aren't really too many other national parks within a reasonable driving distance. However, an alternative to that trip is to see the scenic and historic sights of northern New Mexico. I-25 leading north from Albuquerque provides easy access to many other roads going to such places as Santa Fe, Taos, and the beautiful mountains and forests that are characteristic of this part of the state.

9

Colorado National Monument

Here is a place that is virtually unknown to most people, even those who have done quite a bit of traveling. This is a most perplexing state of affairs for me, because the Colorado National Monument is easily accessible and, more important, is one of the most beautiful sights anywhere in America. Perhaps because of its relative obscurity, the visitor comes away more impressed by its awe-inspiring vistas than would be the case in better-known parks. It will take a prominent place in your memory.

The monument is an impressive example of the effects of wind and rain on the landscape. A masterpiece of nature, the immense monolithic formations have such fanciful names as the Coke Ovens and the Pipe Organ. They rise from a flat canyon over 1,000 feet deep and often reach above the plateau rim from which you will be viewing them.

Facts & Figures

LOCATION/GATEWAYS/GETTING THERE: In the extreme west-central part of Colorado, the monument is conveniently located just three miles south of the Fruita exit of I-70 or by the Monument Road exit in the larger town of Grand Junction. The logical gateway is Denver, which is 260 miles east on I-70, an easy and wonderfully scenic drive of about five hours.

YEAR ESTABLISHED: The Colorado National Monument was proclaimed in 1911.

SIZE: 20,454 acres (or 32 square miles).

ADMISSION FEE: $4.

CLIMATE/WHEN TO GO: A dry, sunny climate in summer, with daytime highs usually in the high 80s or low 90s. The monument is open all year, but the winters are cold and snowy. Because of the high altitude, spring and fall, though usually pleasant, can become unexpectedly cold. Summer is the best time to visit.

ADDRESS/TELEPHONE: Superintendent, Colorado National Monument, Fruita, CO 81521. (303) 858-3617.

Auto Tour/Short Stops

From the casual visitor's perspective, one of the monument's best features is how easy it is to tour it from the comfort of your car. The monument is long and narrow, being traversed by the 23-mile Rim Rock Drive. It is a two-way thoroughfare, but you will exit it from the end opposite where you came in. Although it doesn't really matter which way you proceed, this description will follow a west-to-east route, simply because the visitor center is nearer to the western entrance.

Rim Rock Drive, once you reach the canyon rim, is mostly level but it contains quite a few turns. Nevertheless, it is easy going. The canyon rim ranges in elevation from about 5,700 feet near the visitor center to over 6,600 feet. Since the west and east entrances are at elevations of, respectively, 4,674 and 5,058 feet, you do have to climb up to the canyon rim and descend once again at the end no matter which direction you drive. Getting to the canyon rim at either end is by a long series of relatively easy switchbacks. They are not so hair-raising as to prevent you from admiring the fantastic scenery. Just take it easy and you'll be fine!

Most of the best sights in the monument are from overlooks set right off the road or a walk of less than 100 yards from the many roadside parking areas. There are also three easy trails that are less than a mile long. So let's take a look at Rim Rock Drive in more detail.

Colorado
National Monument

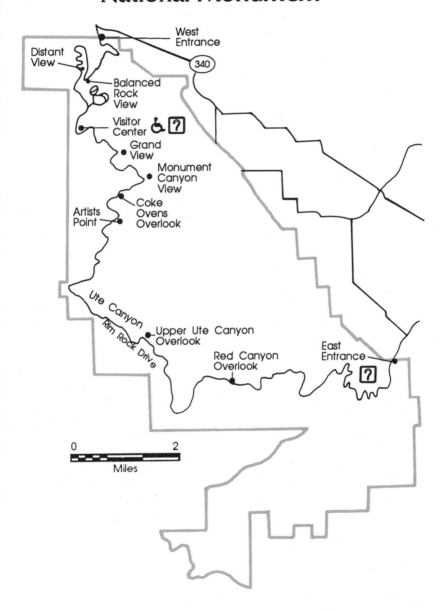

Rising sharply to the canyon rim, you will first reach the **Redlands View** and **Balanced Rock** then, after proceeding through two tunnels and past Fruita Canyon, you will come upon **Distant View**. The first trail then is reached at **Window Rock**, with a one-way length of about one-third of a mile. It is easy to do and will give you a fine view of the Window formation, Monument Canyon and the Grand Valley.

Then you arrive at the visitor center, which has some interesting exhibits and information on the monument's development, geology and activities. Directly behind the visitor center is the **Canyon Rim Trail**. This level, half-mile trail leads to a sheltered overlook from which there is the most magnificent view of Monument Canyon.

Leaving the visitor center, the view stops will come upon you one after the other. **Independence View, Grand View** and **Monument Canyon View** are in quick succession, followed by the **Coke Ovens**. The first three of the above provide expansive views of the broad canyon with the large, eroded rock formations scattered about. The Coke Ovens, grouped together like some metal-working furnace of Paul Bunyon, are easily viewed from the overlook, but there is a trail here as well (see below).

Next comes **Artist Point, Highland View** and **Upper Ute Canyon**, then **Fallen Rock** and **Ute Canyon**. At this point, you will have traveled about 60% of Rim Rock Drive and the view stops will start to be spaced further apart. I should mention that no two are alike and even ones that look out upon the same formation from different vantage points tend to appear entirely different to the viewer. Furthermore, light shadings depending upon where you are standing will have a tremendous affect on what you see.

Red Canyon and **Cold Shivers Point** overlooks will round out the views before the road begins its descent to the east entrance station.

To drive the length of Rim Rock Drive, including time for stopping at the mentioned overlooks and short trails, requires a little over two hours.

Getting Out/Longer Stops

There aren't really that many trails in addition to the ones contained in the Auto Tour, except for several long ones (up to seven miles) that descend into the canyon and are quite strenuous. These are not part of a casual visit to the monument. However, one slightly longer trail is the **Coke Ovens Trail**. It is just under a mile round-trip and takes about 40 minutes. It will bring you right close up to the giant, rounded Coke Oven formations and is worthwhile because it gives you a better idea of just how large the formations in the canyon really are. They look huge from the distance of the canyon rim. Next to them, all but the mightiest skyscrapers would pale by comparison.

Accommodations & Dining

There are no lodging or eating establishments within the monument itself. However, nearby Grand Junction has a variety of independent and chain-affiliated motels and plenty of restaurants of all types.

Where Do We Go From Here?

As Denver is the closest major city, you should consider *Trip 3*, which catches all the scenic and other highlights of Colorado, truly one of America's most beautiful states. But if you are pressed for time, the trip to and from Denver along I-70 passes through the heart of the **Rocky Mountains**, with many resort and historic towns just off the road. And just north of Denver itself is **Rocky Mountain National Park**. Less than two hours south of the Colorado National Monument is the **Black Canyon of the Gunnison National Monument** and the **Curecanti National Recreation Area**.

10

Crater Lake National Park

The deep blue color of Crater Lake has been the objective of many attempted descriptions, but none comes close to the impact you will feel on seeing it for the first time. The first name given to it by non-native Americans was simply "Deep Blue Lake." Perhaps that was not such a bad name, because the best description I can offer is to say that it is the bluest blue in all the world. The blue is a result of the lake's great depth – 1,932 feet at its maximum, which makes it one of the world's deepest. It is 4½ miles wide and six miles long, with a 20-mile shoreline. The dimensions and color are enough to attract visitors, but its setting, surrounded by lava cliffs ranging in height from 500 to 2,000 feet above the lake surface, make it all the more remarkable.

The present mountain, which encompasses Crater Lake, is all that remains of a much larger mountain called Mount Mazama. This former giant reached 12,000 feet before an ancient volcanic eruption caused the mountain top to collapse, creating the huge caldera which is now Crater Lake. While the crater is "the thing" at Crater Lake National Park, and people sometimes just come to stare at it for the whole day, there is a lot more to do and see throughout the park. Let's now take a further look.

Facts & Figures

LOCATION/GATEWAYS/GETTING THERE: Set in the southwestern portion of Oregon, Crater Lake is not close to any large city. It can be reached from I-5 by taking SR 62 at Medford. From US 97 (at the town of Klamath Falls), take SR 62 after it branches off from US 97 just past Modoc Point. Coming from the north via US 97, SR 136 leads to the park's north entrance. The nearest major city is Portland. If you are coming directly from there, take I-5 south to Roseburg and pick up scenic SR 138 eastbound to the park. The total driving time from Portland is about six hours.

YEAR ESTABLISHED: First "discovered" by white explorers in 1853, Crater Lake became a national park in 1902.

SIZE: 183,227 acres (or 268 square miles).

ADMISSION FEE: $5.

CLIMATE/WHEN TO GO: The park is open all year in theory, but the main attraction, the drive around the crater, is covered by the remains of winter's heavy snows until about the middle of July. Most other activities in the park are also restricted to the summer season, especially July and August. The park is certainly the most crowded then, but for a first visit you should definitely plan to go during that time to see it at its most beautiful. Fortunately, summer weather is excellent – most days are sunny and mild.

ADDRESS/TELEPHONE: Superintendent, Crater Lake National Park, Box 7, Crater Lake, OR 97604. (503) 594-2211. If you are planning to come in early July, be sure to call ahead to find out which roads will be open.

Auto Tour/Short Stops

Much of Crater Lake can, fortunately, be seen from your car or in short, easy walks. **Crater Rim Drive** does just as its name implies – it completely encircles the entire crater and its lake. You may pick up Crater Rim Drive from the south and north entrances. For ease of description, this Auto Tour will travel clockwise beginning where the access road from SR 62 reaches the 33-mile Rim Drive at the Steel Information Center. Just beyond this point is **Rim Village,**

Crater Lake National Park

Pumice Desert

Cleetwood Trail

Rim Drive

Crater Lake

Wizard Island

Cloud Cap

Rim Village Visitor Center

Phantom Ship

The Pinnacles

4 MILES

N

the focal point for many activities and is the site of all park services, including lodging and food.

Begin your activities with the visitor center, which has excellent exhibits on the formation of Crater Lake. From here it is a short walk via paved path to the **Sinnot Memorial Overlook**, built in two levels upon a parapet overlooking the lake. Your first view of the lake is likely to be the most impressive, no matter where you begin the tour. However, as you will soon see, no two views are alike because of the variation in the background scenery as well as the way the sunlight hits the water from a particular vantage point. In summer you are almost certain to have ideal viewing conditions, except perhaps during the early morning hours.

Now you can begin your excursion around the lake on the Rim Drive. It is mostly level with some easy grades and numerous, mostly gentle turns. One of the major points you pass is **Hillman Peak**, the highest elevation on the rim at 8,156 feet. Shortly after comes **Llao Rock**, a lava flow rising abruptly from the water and reaching a height of 1,850 feet above the lake. Up ahead is **Cleetwood Cove**, from which there is an excellent overall view of the lake and the surrounding mountains. (There will be more about Cleetwood Cove in the next section.) At **Cloud Cap** you should take the short spur road extending three-quarters of a mile that leads up to this impressive formation, offering one of the very best views of the lake without climbing to the top of a peak. Shortly after Cloud Cap comes **Kerr Notch**, which provides an outstanding view of the **Phantom Ship**. This huge stone outcropping certainly does have the shape of an ancient sea vessel and the lonely, desolate rock would make you believe that its inhabitants could be ghosts.

Right after Kerr Notch is a side road leading down through **Wheeler Canyon**. The round-trip covers about 12 miles. It is one of the lesser known areas of the park, but the dozen extra miles are well worthwhile because along Wheeler Creek Canyon are pumice formations known as **The Pinnacles**. At the far end of the drive they become very numerous. Impressive in size, at nearly 200 feet, but a stark, drab gray color, the pinnacles can be seen from alongside the road. Pullouts are provided. This section of the park offers a brief interlude from the lake scene.

Rejoining Rim Drive, **Sun Notch** provides another excellent, tree-framed view of Crater Lake and the Phantom Ship. Soon you will be back at Rim Village, having completed the loop road. The drive as described with stops for views should take just over two hours.

Getting Out/Longer Stops

If you have more time and are willing to expend a little effort, there is much to see and do. We will again work clockwise from the Rim Visitor Center, where a trail leads to **Garfield Peak**. An easy 1¾-mile ascent to the 8,060-foot summit provides views that are truly magnificient, encompassing the entire lake and Wizard Island. Allow two hours for the round-trip.

The Watchman is another peak and the trail here is shorter and easier than the one just mentioned. It is only a 40-minute walk. Among the sights you'll see from either of these trails is Wizard Island. Although it can be seen well from a number of stops along the Rim Drive, at these higher elevations the view is more impressive.

Cleetwood Cove contains the trail head that leads down to the lake shore itself. It is a bit over a mile long and not so bad going down, but it can be hard going on the return trip. The major reason for taking this trail is that it leads to the boat dock where two-hour lake trips begin ($). These excursions stop at **Wizard Island**, the largest island in the lake. Wizard is itself another cinder cone with trails leading to the top of it. If you do this hike you will have to return on a later boat. The trips are hourly from 9:00 am until 3:00 pm, June to September.

Near the SR 62 entrance is the **Godfrey Glen Trail**. This is a level and easy one-mile trail that takes 30-40 minutes and passes through heavily forested areas and numerous small canyons with pinnacle-type formations. If you did not venture down Wheeler Canyon on the Auto Tour, then this trail is a must. The adjacent **Annie Creek Trail** is slightly longer and traverses a small canyon.

Accommodations & Dining

Crater Lake Lodge, with 80 rooms, is the major overnight facility in the park. It consists of both lodge rooms and rustic cottages (M). Smaller **Mazama Lodge** (M) is near the south entrance. If you are going to be taking the boat ride on Crater Lake it is likely that your visit to the park will extend overnight; if so, reserve far in advance to be sure room is available at the lodge. The nearest accommodations outside of the park are 50 miles away in either Klamath Falls or in Medford.

The lodge has two restaurants for those wanting a full meal. The **Rim Village** has a cafeteria and snack bar.

Where Do We Go From Here?

Crater Lake is not close to anything else described in this book, but it is most logically part of a loop trip through Oregon and nearby points in Washington and California as described in *Trip 9*. If your trip is to be a shorter one (probably originating and ending in Portland), you should consider coming south from Portland on I-5 and, after seeing Crater Lake, taking in the beautiful Oregon Coast on the return trip.

11

Craters of the Moon National Monument

Only in Hawaii will you be able to find a greater number of volcanic formations comprised of basalt than there are at Craters of the Moon. Here, a number of eruptions ages ago and huge rivers of molten lava gushing out from a rift in the earth have created immense fields of hardened lava, dotted with many thousands of cinder cones and deep crater-like depressions. So much is the surface like that on the moon, that astronauts in the Apollo program were brought here to get a better idea of the type of landscape they would encounter on the moon itself.

The last known eruptions in this area took place over 2,000 years ago. They have left a legacy for all to see. When it was first discovered by explorers, the area was described as a "desolate, awful waste." Although this may be quite true from an agricultural standpoint (even though you will find various shrubs and plants here and there), it is not a waste to the human eye which can, even in these rather eerie surroundings, find a certain beauty in it all. It is different enough to be called "out of this world."

Facts & Figures

LOCATION/GATEWAYS/GETTING THERE: In the south-central portion of Idaho, the monument is on US 20/26/93, about 80 miles west of Idaho Falls and 180 miles east of Boise via I-84 to US 26. Boise provides the nearest adequate scheduled airline service. Salt

Lake City is another alternative. It is, however, more than 200 miles away via I-15 and US 26.

YEAR ESTABLISHED: First explored as early as 1833, the area was designated as a national monument in 1924.

SIZE: 53,545 acres (or 84 square miles).

ADMISSION FEE: $4.

CLIMATE/WHEN TO GO: The monument road is open from late April to early November, which presents a small problem: the summer is quite hot, but the spring and fall are a bit chilly for seeing some of the relatively nearby national parks that will probably be combined with your visit to the Craters of the Moon. So, unless you are specifically coming to see this monument, you'll have to put up with a mid-summer sun that brings temperatures well into the 90s and frequently higher. It is, fortunately, a dry climate. Try to visit during the morning hours.

ADDRESS/TELEPHONE: Superintendent, Craters of the Moon National Monument, P.O. Box 29, Arco, ID 83213. (208) 527-3257.

Auto Tour/Short Stops

Virtually all of the monument's major features are easily accessible via a seven-mile loop road that begins from near the entrance station. First stop into the **Craters of the Moon Visitor Center** for a good orientation about the monument and a description of its very active geologic past. Now you will be ready to begin the loop.

A short trail leads to the summit of **Inferno Cone**, from which there is a good view of the surrounding terrain. Some of the strangest features in this area are "lava bombs," which were pieces of lava hurled out by the force of volcanic action. These hardened pieces range in size from a mere quarter of an inch to several feet across.

Next comes a good view of **Big Cinder Butte**, which is over 800 feet high and is the largest volcanic formation in the monument. After this is an area known as the **Big Craters - Spatter Cones**. This is the section that is probably the most "moon-like." From here there is a short trail to the cave area (see next section).

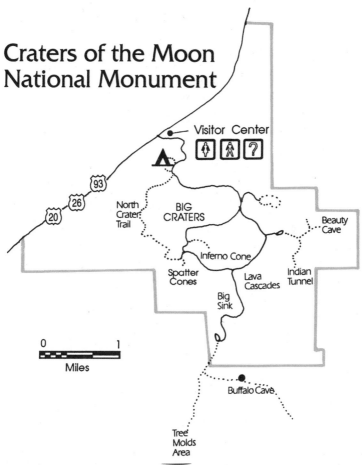

Craters of the Moon National Monument

Visitor Center

North Crater Trail

BIG CRATERS

Beauty Cave

Inferno Cone

Spatter Cones

Lava Cascades

Indian Tunnel

Big Sink

0   1
Miles

Buffalo Cave

Tree Molds Area

Just ahead now on the loop is the beginning of another fairly short trail, this time to the **Devil's Orchard** – so-called because it contains a sizable amount of vegetation (sorry, no orchards) compared to the mostly barren landscape elsewhere along the route. It also provides a panorama of the monument's largest field of cinder cones. Another short trail leads to the **Tree Mold Area**, where lava hardened around the outside of living trees, leaving an empty shell in its place through the passage of time.

The loop now brings you back to the visitor center and the exit from the monument. As the several trails mentioned are all short (ranging from 10 to 30 minutes at most), and the drive is extremely brief, you should be able to complete the Auto Tour in two hours or less.

Getting Out/Longer Stops

Longer, strenuous trails are in the interior of the monument, off the loop road by a long hike. These are not for the casual visitor. You might want to take the trail to the **Cave Area**. This contains a number of lava tubes formed when the cooling of lava on the outside of the flow allowed hotter, still molten lava on the inside to pass through, leaving a pipe-like tube. Some of these measure as much as 50 feet across while the longest, Indian Tunnel, is 830 feet from end to end. But most are much smaller. You can explore several of them, but bring along a flashlight and wear sturdy shoes. Summer visitors might want to carry water as well. Exploration of a few tubes and the trail to and from the area can take over an hour.

Accommodations & Dining

There are no lodging facilities within the monument nor in the immediate vicinity. The nearest decent concentration of facilities is in Idaho Falls (80 miles east) and Shoshone (about 64 miles west). But since touring time is well under a half-day, you should have no trouble arranging your itinerary to get to one of these places or beyond. If you must have something to quiet your tummy right before or after your visit, the small town of Arco (19 miles east) does have some places that will keep you from starving.

Where Do We Go From Here?

Suggested Trip 5 includes Craters of the Moon National Monument along with several major national parks. If you are interested in a shorter trip, however, with Boise as your base, you can visit this monument, the **Sawtooth National Recreation Area** and **Hells Canyon National Recreation Area**.

A few extra words about nearby Hells Canyon are required. This is certainly an area of exceptional beauty and was only grudgingly excluded from this book because it is very hard to reach – the roads are generally very difficult, if not hazardous for the inexperienced mountain driver. In addition, the area is toured mostly by boat, rather than by car. If you are in the vicinity, jet boat tours of the canyon can be taken up the Snake River from several towns not far from Boise. Contact 1-(800)-422-3568 for additional information.

12

Devils Tower
National Monument

Long before it gained additional notoriety from the motion picture *Close Encounters of the Third Kind*, Devils Tower was one of the most recognizable landmarks, not only in Wyoming, but in the entire country. It is not difficult to understand why. Rising 867 feet (1,267 feet above the Belle Fourche River), this gigantic monolith is visible, on clear days, from as much as 100 miles away!

Some other statistics are equally staggering. It is estimated to be 50 million years old. At the bottom it is almost 1,000 feet across, but it narrows as it rises so that at the very top it covers an area of only about 1½ acres. Although many people climb it (we're told that it is much easier than it looks), you won't be doing so as a casual visitor. However, in case you are wondering what's on top (besides a view of the surrounding plain and the distant Black Hills), it is covered with grass and sagebrush – something of an anticlimax.

The tower itself is quite beautiful, having been described most often as a gigantic stone tree stump. And, indeed, its many fluted columns do give that effect. But however you picture it, it is certainly among the most unusual of the many geologic formations in the country.

Facts & Figures

LOCATION/GATEWAYS/GETTING THERE: In the northeastern corner of Wyoming, the tower is about 110 miles northwest of Rapid City, South Dakota via I-90 to Sundance, then by US 14 and SR 24. It is 300 miles from Billings, Montana via I-90 to Moorcroft, then US 14 and SR 24 again.

YEAR ESTABLISHED: The first ascent of the monolith was made in 1893. It became America's first national monument in 1906.

SIZE: 1,347 acres (or 2 square miles), making it one of the smallest scenic attractions administered by the National Park Service.

ADMISSION FEE: $4.

CLIMATE/WHEN TO GO: This area has four distinct seasons. Although the monument is open all year, the summer is warm, generally dry and very sunny, providing the best conditions for seeing it from a distance as well as close up.

ADDRESS/TELEPHONE: Superintendent, Devils Tower National Monument, Devils Tower, WY 82714. (307) 467-5283.

Auto Tour/Getting Out

We'll combine the two categories because, obviously, in an area this small you will not be doing a lot of driving. In some ways you will see Devil's Tower better before you arrive than once you are there! The feeling as you approach it is awesome. It just keeps growing until, when you are right on top of it, you have to strain your neck to glimpse the top.

About a half-mile inside the entrance station you will come to a prairie dog colony, one of the largest of the few remaining in the country. Although they live in underground burrows, you can recognize the entrances to their homes, which look almost like small volcanic cinder cones. If you are lucky, you may see quite a few of these cute, squirrel-like animals scampering about. Don't feed them or try to touch them, however. They will generally run away but will bite if cornered.

Devils Tower National Monument

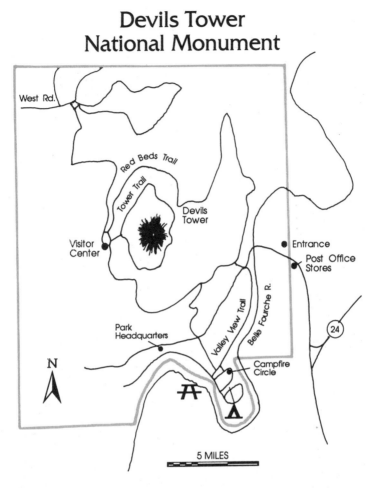

Another 2½ miles along the road will bring you to **Devil's Tower Visitor Center**, where there are exhibits about pioneers as well as information on the history of Devils Tower. From here begins the trail that encircles this monumental rock. It is actually a mile-long nature trail, resplendent with its many varieties of plants and flowers, but your eyes will constantly be drawn to the tower, which stands like a sentinel above you.

Your visit to Devils Tower should take under 2½ hours, with the walk around it included.

Special Activities

Although we haven't generally mentioned talks by rangers in other chapters, there is one that is especially interesting here and you should make every effort to attend. This is the demonstration by Park Rangers of **how to climb Devils Tower**. The demos are given frequently, especially in summer, and yes, you can simply watch and will not be forced to scale the giant beast!

Accommodations & Dining

The nearest towns with lodging available are Hulett (10 miles north) and Sundance (about 28 miles south). The latter has a greater selection. Restaurants can be found somewhat closer, especially in the direction of Sundance. Depending upon your route, the proximity of the Black Hills region gives you plenty of alternative places to seek food and, especially, lodging.

Where Do We Go From Here?

As just mentioned, Devils Tower is very close to the **Black Hills**. Therefore, it is logical to consider *Trip 2* described in the last section of this book. However, the trip across Wyoming via US 14/16 to **Yellowstone** on the opposite side of the state is one of the most scenic rides in the nation, particularly in the western half of the state. So you may want to compose a trip that, while still taking in the Black Hills, does all of northern Wyoming as well. Some of the cities of southern Montana can serve as alternative gateways for such an adventure.

13

Everglades National Park

One may wonder how a vast area with a maximum variation in elevation of less than 25 feet can be considered scenic. Well, the Everglades National Park may not have the spectacular scenery found in some of the other parks, but it does have a tranquil beauty that is unique. The largest subtropical wilderness area in the nation, the park is essentially a broad river (averaging some 50 miles wide) that is, remarkably, only a few inches deep. This very shallow fresh water, moving much more slowly than a "normal" river, contributes to the development of marsh and mangrove. It supports an enormous variety of flora and fauna, including many different species of palms and sawgrass. It is home for crocodiles and alligators, to mention just two animals that visitors are always eager to see here.

Nowhere else in the continental states, not even in the bayou country of Louisiana, will you find a tropical world such as this. So, come along on our trip to a land from another era.

Facts & Figures

LOCATION/GATEWAYS/GETTING THERE: In the extreme southwestern corner of Florida, the park is under 40 miles from Miami via US 1 and SR 9336, making it the only national park of comparable size located so close to a major city. It can also be reached from the Tampa/St. Petersburg area, a distance of approximately 200 miles by I-75 and US 41 (the Tamiami Trail).

YEAR ESTABLISHED: The remnant of what was once a much larger area of wilderness, the park was established in 1934 to prevent further encroachment of development.

SIZE: 1,398,937 acres (or 2,186 square miles), making the Everglades larger than Delaware and one of the biggest parks in the entire country.

ADMISSION FEE: $5.

CLIMATE/WHEN TO GO: Being in southern Florida makes it possible to carry on outdoor activities at any time of the year. However, the summer is extremely hot and humid despite cooling coastal breezes; mosquitos are another summer problem. From mid-September through mid-November certain activities may be cancelled because of high-water conditions. This, too, is hurricane season in the gulf and along the Atlantic seaboard. December through May is the ideal time to visit.

ADDRESS/TELEPHONE: Superintendent, Everglades National Park, Box 279, Homestead, FL 33030. (305) 247-7700.

Auto Tour/Short Stops

The park can be entered at one of three access points. Two of them (at Everglades City and at Shark Valley) are off US 41 on the park's northern edge. These, however, are away from the main area of sights and are not part of the Auto Tour. They will be described under Special Activities.

The main driving route into the park is via SR 9336, just east of Florida City on Route US 1. A road extends from the entrance at Parachute Key to Flamingo, a one-way distance of 36 miles. Most of the attractions are along this route.

Begin at the main visitor center just inside the entrance. There is a lot of information on the park here, but even more is available at the nearby **Royal Palm Interpretive Center**, located at the end of a short side road. From this spot begins the **Anhinga Trail**, an elevated boardwalk that gives visitors the best opportunity to view much of the wildlife, (including alligators, found in the park.

Everglades National Park

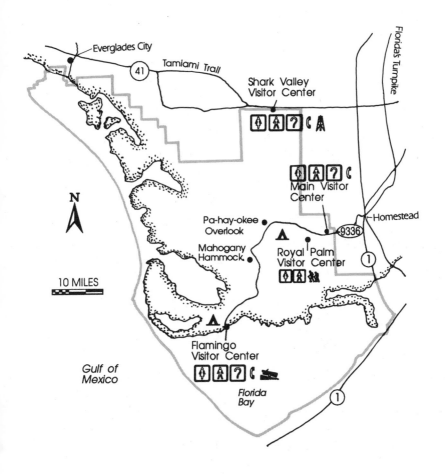

Also starting here is the **Gumbo Limbo Trail**, which highlights the abundant jungle-like plant life. The starting points for this trail and most of the others are a short ride off the main road. Some of these may take a bit longer than we usually allow for inclusion in the Auto Tour, but since they are all level, easy trails that do not take a great deal of time, we are including them here.

Soon after, you come upon the **Pine Key Nature Trail** and then the **Pinelands Trail**. Both have many more examples of trees that are native to the park.

Your next stop is at the **Pa-hay-okee Overlook**. The 12-foot-high tower provides a panoramic view of the southern portion of the Shark River Basin, a vast wilderness area teeming with sawgrass. This plant gets its name from its razor-sharp leaves – sharp enough to tear your clothes or your skin. Don't touch sawgrass if you encounter it along any of the trails.

A few miles further down the road is **Mahogany Hammock**. Here is another easy, elevated boardwalk. The trail will take you through an area of mahogany trees and various subtropical plant species. The next boardwalk is the **Mangrove Trail**, a lush mangrove forest penetrated by the raised wooden walkway.

The last trail is at **West Lake**. Here you can wander along the water's edge by a mangrove forest. About 15 miles later you reach the end of the road at Flamingo. Here are numerous recreational and other visitor facilities. Flamingo is on Cape Sable, the southernmost point of the U.S. mainland.

The stopping points have been listed in the order that you will reach them driving towards Flamingo. However, if you skip some on the way in, that will leave you something to see on the return trip. As the trails are short and easy, your Auto Tour will take about five hours to complete, round-trip.

Getting Out/Longer Stops

Other than the trails mentioned above, there are really no other opportunities for walks along the Auto Tour. But you can extend your visit on most of them by staying a bit longer and scanning the surrounding area for wildlife. Your patience will often be rewarded.

Special Activities

There are a number of very popular activities in the Everglades. First, at the Shark Valley entrance there is a 2½-hour guided tram tour of the **Shark Valley** area ($). This is one of the thickest areas of vegetation in the park (largely sawgrass), and a half-hour stop is made at a high observation tower so that you can take in the scenery and look for wildlife. The view of the valley area is much better here than the one described previously for the Pa-hay-okee Overlook. Tours are often unavailable from the middle of September until the middle of November because of high water conditions. Private cars are never allowed on the 15-mile tram route.

There are numerous **bicycle tours** and **canoe trips** that begin in Flamingo. Boat trips also depart from Flamingo several times daily, with reduced operations from June 1st through the end of October ($). The Everglades City entrance provides access to the waterways of the Everglades for those who have brought along their own boats. However, as the labyrinth of "canals" can be very confusing, plan any such excursion carefully with the aid of charts available from the Everglades City Ranger Station. If you have a small boat, you might try the special "Canoe Trails" located along the road. They vary in length from four to 16 miles. These are shorter than the waterways of the Wilderness Waterway area and you're less likely to get lost on them.

Finally, **airboats**, which skim along the water's surface, are a popular means of touring the interior of the Everglades. These trips are available from a number of private operators ($). Many of them can be found along the Tamiami Trail from west of Miami to near the park. Such trips vary from a few hours to the better part of a day.

Accommodations

The Flamingo Lodge at Flamingo has motel-type accommodations for those wishing to stay in the park (M). More varied facilities are near the main entrance of the park in the towns of Homestead and Florida City. However, if you will be seeing the park as a day trip out of Miami, you will definitely have more choice in the city.

Dining

Besides a full-service restaurant at Flamingo, a snack shop will be found here as well. Everything from fast food to gourmet meals is available within a short distance of the park entrance.

Where Do We Go From Here?

Although there are many beautiful gardens and natural springs nearby, such as **Weeki Wachi, Homosassa** and **Silver Springs**, there are few national parks. The Everglades can be included with a number of excursions in central or southern Florida. Its proximity to Miami makes it an excellent day trip for people soaking up the sun along the nearby ocean beaches. It is also near the beginning of the lovely Overseas Highway to Key West. Related natural attractions are close by as well. **Biscayne National Park** is less than 25 miles away. It preserves a coral reef formation. Boat trips are offered. **John Pennekamp Coral Reef State Park** at Key Largo is a similar area. Finally, it is not that far from central Florida, home of **Walt Disney World, Cape Canaveral** and so many other attractions that it would take a separate chapter just to list them. So, have fun!

14

Glacier National Park

The worst thing you can say about Glacier is that it doesn't quite have the diversity of features found in, for example, Yellowstone, Yosemite, or Olympic National Park. But, what it does have in abundance is the finest mountain scenery in the country. The terrain is highlighted by over 50 major glaciers and more than 200 lakes. Top that off with a tremendous variety of trees and all colors of wildflowers in summer, and you have a natural setting par excellence.

Probably the highlight of the park for most visitors is the famous "Going to the Sun Road," an engineering marvel that crosses the Continental Divide at an elevation of 6,680 feet and provides access to some of the park's outstanding scenery.

This majestic area extends beyond the northern edge of the park into Canada. Wisely, the United States and Canada have created an international park here. Together, the two parks form Waterton Lakes-Glacier International Peace Park. A special section on Waterton Lakes is found at the end of this chapter.

There is a special tranquillity here in the rarefied mountain air. And beauty everywhere. A visit will not soon be forgotten.

Facts & Figures

LOCATION/GATEWAYS/GETTING THERE: In the northwestern part of Montana, the park is accessible from the western side via US 2 to West Glacier and from the east via US 89. It is 170 miles from Great Falls via I-15 and US 2/89 or 275 miles from Spokane, Washington via US 2. Missoula is the closest gateway, 150 miles south of the park via US 93 and US 2. Each has commercial airline service available.

YEAR ESTABLISHED: Glacier became a national park in 1910.

SIZE: 1,013,595 acres (or 1,584 square miles).

ADMISSION FEE: $5.

CLIMATE/WHEN TO GO: Since the entire Going to the Sun Road is only open from mid-June to mid-October, a first-time visitor should plan on visiting during this period. Note that trailers are banned from crossing the park on Going to the Sun Road during July and August. The summer weather is excellent: comfortable temperatures with cool mornings and evenings, plenty of sunshine and infrequent rain. A light jacket is advisable, even in mid-summer. In early summer the wildflowers are at their glorious peak.

ADDRESS/TELEPHONE: Superintendent, Glacier National Park, West Glacier, MT 59936. (406) 888-5441.

Auto Tour/Short Stops

Although many of the park's largest glaciers are in the back-country and are, therefore, accessible only to overnight hikers, even from the road and short trails there is almost too much beauty for most people to absorb.

The major portion of the park is traversed by the Going to the Sun Road. We'll work our way from the West Glacier entrance eastward to the St. Mary's entrance. You can do it the other way as well but, if you do, be sure to work out when you will see the attractions in the other sections of this park (in this routing they are given at the end of the Auto Tour).

The road has 17 scenic overlooks. I'll dispense with the normal practice of noting the best ones and urge you to stop at all of them because each is truly majestic. And since the course of this wonderful highway will take you a distance of some 50 miles, 17 stops are not as many as you might think at first.

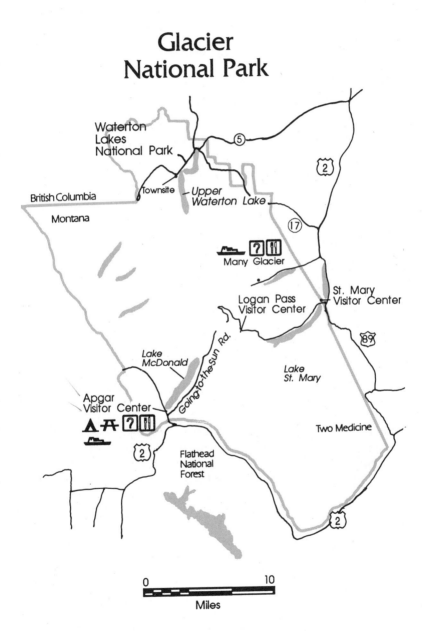

Just inside the west entrance the roadway runs along **Lake Mac-Donald** which, at 10 miles long and a mile across, is the park's largest lake. The heavily forested shoreline is set against a backdrop of lofty 6,000-foot mountains. As soon as you get past the lake, the road begins its dramatic climb toward the Continental Divide.

At the Avalanche Creek parking area you should make a stop to explore the ¼-mile **Trail of the Cedars**. This is a boardwalk trail and is very easy, taking no more than 15 minutes. During the course of this walk you will see beautiful trees and a rushing river. Another trail from here goes on to Avalanche Creek itself, a deep and narrow gorge with stunning views from the trail. An even longer continuation of this trail is described in the following section.

Resume the breathtaking climb around a section of the road called The Loop and head towards the Continental Divide at **Logan Pass**, which is about half-way through the park. On the way you will come across many areas where the road has a precipitous drop off the edge of the mountain on one side and on the other, a sheer wall of rock. Often you will see water from melting snow cascading down these rock walls and onto the roadway. It is both an unusual and beautiful sight. Even during the middle of summer there are patches of snow everywhere. It is also in this area that the road is at its most dramatic – switchbacks give you dizzying views of mountain peaks and the road ahead and behind, above and below.

The park's main visitor center is at the Logan Pass itself. It has interesting exhibits and is the starting point for many guided walks as well as self-guiding trails (to be described later).

Upon leaving Logan Pass the road will start winding its way downward and you will soon reach the beginning of St. Mary's Lake. At **Sun Point**, after a spectacular whirlwind descent, one of the park's most beautiful vistas will unfold before you. Here, too, is a short trail to majestic **Baring Falls**. Then, when you reach the far end of the lake you'll be at the **St. Mary's Visitor Center** and the eastern entrance of the park.

Many people feel that, having seen all of this, their visit to Glacier is complete. But this would be an unfortunate mistake, because there is much more. About 10 miles north of St. Mary's on US 89, at the town of Babb, there is a 13-mile road that leads back into the park. This area is known as the **Many Glacier Region**. At the end of the road is **Swiftcurrent Lake** and, with its mountain setting, it is certainly one of the most impressive areas in the entire park.

There are many trails leading from the end of the road (see next section).

Then return to Babb. You can head south, but I strongly suggest heading north, via the Chief Mountain International Highway. This detour will not only take you through the fantastic scenery of Glacier Park's **Belly River Country** (an area especially popular among back-packers, but it can also be appreciated from the road); it also provides direct access to Canada's **Waterton Lakes National Park**. Details on Waterton are provided at the end of this chapter.

Now you can head back south, picking up US 89 once again and taking it to SR 49 and the Two Medicine entrance of Glacier in the park's southeastern corner. Here, at the end of a short road, are a beautiful lake, more majestic mountain peaks and one of the deepest and most impressive valleys in the park. There is a short trail to beautiful **Twin Falls**.

Time allocation for your Auto Tour depends on whether or not you will be making all of the side trips. The Going to the Sun Road portion can be accomplished in about four hours. Allow another two hours to visit the Many Glacier region. Then, it is over an hour to Two Medicine, and you should allow another half-hour once there. So, even without an extension to Waterton Lakes, the complete Auto Tour of Glacier will take a minimum of seven hours.

Getting Out/Longer Stops

There are numerous additional trails that don't require back-country hiking. Past Avalanche Gorge there is a four-mile trail to **Avalanche Lake and Basin**, probably one of the more beautiful spots in the entire park, where you will stand at the lake shore surrounded by rocky mountains. It does require almost three hours, but if there is one really long trail that you are considering, this should definitely be it. The trail, despite its length, is not at all difficult.

From the Logan Pass Visitor Center the **Hanging Gardens Trail** extends along a feature known as the **Garden Wall**, which is really a section of the Continental Divide. The views are simply wonderful. You don't have to do the entire three-mile, two-hour trail. Even a relatively small portion of it will give you an excellent idea of what it is like. You will be walking on some snow along this trail even in the middle of summer, so dress appropriately. There is a long boardwalk behind the visitor center leading towards giant rock formations. This is part of the trail to beautiful **Hidden Lake** (1½ miles each way). Diverse topography, including meadows and a glacial morraine, will be encountered along the way.

Finally, in the Many Glacier area there are numerous trails surrounding Swiftcurrent Lake. It is advisable at least to walk around part of the lakeside trail to see the deep green water from various angles with its different backgrounds of gray mountains and icy glaciers.

Special Activities

There are day-long **bus tours** of the park that depart from various hotels within the park ($), but it is really better to do it on your own. In addition, there are boat rides on Lake MacDonald, St. Mary and Swiftcurrent Lakes ranging from one to two hours. **Boat rentals** are also available for those who wish to go on their own ($). From the town of West Glacier there are **float** and **whitewater trips** on the middle fork of the Flathead River, which forms the southwestern border of the park. These trips, which vary from several hours to all day, go into areas that are not near the park's road system, so they have a big advantage over the lake boat rides ($).

You can also add some driving and skirt the southern boundary of the park between West Glacier and East Glacier via US 2. The scenery along the Flathead River and by 5,220-foot-high Marias Pass is beautiful, but is not a substitute for the Going To The Sun Road.

Accommodations

Because of the time it takes to see the park, you will have to spend at least one night within the park itself or in the immediate area. Most park accommodations are modest, but clean and comfortable; they are all in beautiful settings. The choices are the **Apgar Village Lodge** near East Glacier, which has 49 cottages (M); **Glacier Park Lodge**, a 155-room lodge at East Glacier Park (E); **Lake MacDonald Lodge**, containing lodge and motel units as well as cabins among its 101 rooms (M to E); the **Many Glacier Hotel**, a 210-room hotel (no elevator in this four-story structure) (E); the **Rising Sun Motor Inn**, seven miles west of the St. Mary entrance, with 71 rooms (M); the **Swiftcurrent Motor Inn** located at Many Glacier with 62 motel-type rooms (M); and the **Village Inn** at Apgar with 36 motel rooms (M to E) . There are also motels right outside the park in the towns of East Glacier Park and West Glacier Park.

All in-park accommodation reservations are through Glacier Park, Inc. Their number is (406) 226-5551 in summer and (602) 207-6000 in winter.

If you are going to be staying in Waterton Lakes National Park, the town has a wide variety of accommodations. The historic **Prince of Wales Hotel** overlooking the lake is worth seeing, even if you decide not to stay there.

Dining

Every place listed above has at least one dining facility except for the Village Inn at Apgar. The Rising Sun and Swiftcurrent Motor Inns have cafeterias; the others all have full-service restaurants. Lake MacDonald Lodge has a coffee shop in addition to its restaurant.

Where Do We Go From Here?

Trip 5, a fabulous scenic adventure, includes Glacier National Park. However, an interesting alternative, especially if you are going to be making a visit to Waterton Lakes, is to head north into Canada and visit the four national parks that comprise the heart of the Canadian Rockies – **Banff, Jasper, Kootenay** and **Yoho**. Those four could take up a book by themselves.

Waterton Lakes National Park

It is wise to include Waterton on any visit to Glacier. The parks are so closely associated with one another that if you write to Glacier Park's Superintendent for information they will include brochures on Waterton even if you don't ask for them.

After arriving via the Chief Mountain International Highway, you will be in Waterton town site. Like many Canadian parks, Waterton has a quaint and picturesque community set in the park itself. These towns are always the focal points for visitor centers, museums, accommodations and services of all kinds. Within the town is a short trail leading to beautiful **Cameron Falls**.

The main feature of your visit to Waterton is likely to be one of the two-hour boat rides ($) on spectacular Waterton Lake itself, a mountain-surrounded jewel. These cruises make a brief stop at **Goat Haunt**, which is actually back in the USA. It is in the northern part of Glacier Park and, except for this boat access, is only available to overnight hikers.

You should also take the drive through **Red Rock Canyon**, where the narrow valley is flanked by high, precipitous red spire-like mountains.

A proper trip to Waterton should take at least four to five hours and, with the travel time there and back to Glacier, will add exactly one day to your Glacier National Park excursion.

15

Glen Canyon & Rainbow Bridge

This vast, state-sized recreation area is a direct consequence of the completion of the Glen Canyon Dam, which backs up manmade Lake Powell for 186 miles. There are plenty of water-related recreational opportunities to attract thousands of visitors. The natural beauty of the area is an impressive array of hidden canyons, coves, and small inlets, with towering red cliffs enclosing the lake shore.

Rainbow Bridge National Monument, a small enclave surrounded on all four sides by the Glen Canyon Recreation Area, certainly must be included among the greatest of all natural wonders of the world. Its symmetry, grace and size defy logic. That it can remain standing seems impossible.

An area with few roads, it has nevertheless been included in this book because some of the best sights are accessible to the visitor coming by car although, as you will see, a boat trip is necessary to truly appreciate the beauty of this rugged country.

Facts & Figures

LOCATION/GATEWAYS/GETTING THERE: In the southern part of Utah and extending into northern Arizona, Glen Canyon is 285 miles north of Phoenix via I-17 and US 89. It is about 275 miles from Las Vegas in an east/northeasterly direction via I-15, Utah SR 9 and US 89.

YEAR ESTABLISHED: The recreation area was officially established in 1972. Rainbow Bridge has been a national monument since 1910.

SIZE: 1,236,880 acres (or 1,933 square miles), similar in size to the state of Delaware. On the other hand, Rainbow Bridge is only 160 acres, equivalent to only a fourth of a square mile.

ADMISSION FEES: There is no charge for entering either area.

CLIMATE/WHEN TO GO: This is an area that can be visited during any season. The winters are pleasantly warm, while the spring and fall aren't too hot. Summer, of course, sees daily high temperature readings of around 100° but, since much of your time visiting here will be spent on the water, even the summer heat is generally tolerable, especially with the low humidity that is typical of the southwest desert areas. However, if you do visit in summer, plan most of your outdoor activities for the morning.

ADDRESS/TELEPHONE: Information on both areas can be obtained from the Superintendent, Glen Canyon National Recreation Area, Box 1507, Page, AZ 86040. (602) 645-8200.

Auto Tour/Getting Out

We will combine these two headings for this chapter because the lack of a road system means that most of your visit will be comprised of attractions described under the Special Activities heading. Your main "base" will be in the town of Page, where US 89 crosses the recreation area. But do take a short side-trip via US 89A to Marble Canyon, where there is an excellent view of the Colorado River way below the high suspension bridge. You should also be aware that SR 95 in the southeastern part of Utah crosses the recreation area as well. However, this area is generally remote (though some of you might come this way as a back route into the Canyonlands) and the scenery is similar to that found in the more accessible regions near Page. The facilities near Page are much more extensive, too. So, unless your route requires using SR 95, it isn't an essential part of touring Glen Canyon.

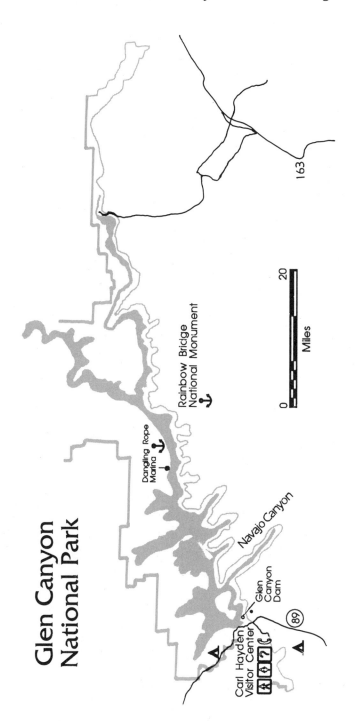

Glen Canyon
National Park

Dangling Rope
Marina

Rainbow Bridge
National Monument

Navajo Canyon

Glen Canyon
Dam

89

Carl Hayden
Visitor Center

163

0   20

Miles

Special Activities

The Carl Hayden Visitor Center in Page is adjacent to the **Glen Canyon Dam** and has information and exhibits on the dam, the area and the geology of the surrounding countryside. Moreover, tours of the dam (either self-guided or via frequent guided tours) leave from this point. The power house and other features are quite interesting, but the best part is going down to the base of the dam, which offers a very different view than those from the observation deck. What you will see from both are the sheer, dark red walls of the Colorado River canyon – so steep that the sunlight hardly reaches the bottom, giving the river a dark, almost black appearance. The suspension bridge which carries US 89 over the river and canyon is also an impressive sight from down below. The view looking up gives a better idea of just how deep the canyon is. Canyon viewpoints are also available from near the south side of the bridge.

As beautiful as this area is, the probable highlight of your visit will be a boat trip on Lake Powell to **Rainbow Bridge National Monument** ($). The monument is accessible only by boat (unless you take a difficult all-day hike through the canyon). There are all-day and half-day (five-hour) cruises ($). The all-day trip goes farther down Lake Powell and visits a few side canyons but, since the scenery beyond Rainbow Bridge is similar to the beginning of the trip, the half-day voyage is the better choice unless you really have a lot of time available. Cruises leave from the Wahweap Marina, a few miles north of Page, early in the morning, returning at around noon; and at one in the afternoon with return in the early evening. From the boat you will see not only the clean, refreshingly cool-looking blue waters of Lake Powell, but also the towering red cliffs that surround the lake. Your captain will point out some of the more notable landmarks, including Navajo Mountain (which bears a resemblance to Devils Tower) and some odd rock formations that look like an enormous dragon. A side canyon will bring you to the boat dock at Rainbow Bridge National Monument. From the dock it is only a 10-minute walk to the bridge which, as it gets closer, becomes more dramatic. The largest such natural bridge in the world, Rainbow Bridge is 290 feet above the river bed and 275 feet across. Do walk directly beneath it and gaze upward for a most unusual view. It is nature's version of the Gateway Arch in St. Louis!

Additional activities at the recreation area are related to the lake –
beaches, swimming, boating, etc. A very popular way of vacation-
ing here is to rent a houseboat and sail around for a few days or
more. Although I have never personally done this, it looks like it
would be fun and an ideal mid-winter vacation.

Accommodations

In addition to scores of motels and motor inns in the town of Page,
there are two resorts within the recreation area (both in the
Wahweap area). These are the small (24-room) **Lake Powell Motel**
(M), and the larger, beautiful **Wahweap Lodge**. With 269 excellent
rooms (E), the lodge has a complete range of recreation facilities
within its expansive grounds. Reservations for both places can be
made through Del Webb Enterprises. This also applies to houseboat rentals and cruises to Rainbow Bridge. Reserve all well in
advance.

Dining

Wahweap Lodge has two excellent restaurants, one of which has a
fantastic breakfast buffet. There is also a fast-food type restaurant
within the complex. No meals are available on the half-day boat
rides, although free refreshments are served. On the full-day cruise,
lunch is included.

Where Do We Go From Here?

These two areas are both included in *Suggested Trip 6*, which covers
many attractions in the state of Arizona. Las Vegas-based trips
provide another alternative. Such a trip can be planned around
southern Utah's national parks and the North Rim of the **Grand
Canyon**; they can be extended to include Glen Canyon and Rainbow Bridge.

16

Grand Canyon National Park

Grand. As in huge, as in great, as in stupendous. There is no single word that better describes the Grand Canyon than its very name. The English author J.B. Priestley said of the Grand Canyon that "those who have not seen it will not believe any possible description. Those who have seen it know that it cannot be described." Its worldwide fame is attested to by the staggering number of foreign visitors who make it a "must see" on their visits to America. Just what is it that makes the Grand Canyon one of the most spectacular sights in all the world?

Certainly size is one factor. It is 277 miles long and ranges from four to 21 miles wide. From the top of the rim to the canyon floor it is 5,700 feet on the north, and 4,500 feet on the south side. Imagine looking down a drop of a mile or more! When you stand on the observation deck of a 100-story building you are only one fourth as high as at the rim of the Grand Canyon. Its colors are another factor. Every shade in the color spectrum seems to be represented, but the beautiful purple shading is probably the most impressive. Its geological significance is a final factor. In its uncountable layers are represented the natural history of the earth – a scientific treasure chest.

Facts & Figures

LOCATION/GATEWAYS/GETTING THERE: Grand Canyon National Park, at the South Rim, is a leisurely 4½-hour drive north of Phoenix via I-17 and US 180. The terrain is relatively flat as you approach the canyon, another factor in its dramatic impact upon first sight. The park covers a significant portion of north-central Arizona.

YEAR ESTABLISHED: European explorers of the Coronado expedition first sighted the canyon in 1540. The 1870 explorations of Major John Powell helped build its reputation and led to creation of the national park in 1919.

SIZE: 1,218,375 acres (or 1,904 square miles).

ADMISSION FEE: $10.

CLIMATE/WHEN TO GO: Because the canyon rim elevations range from 5,000 to more than 9,000 feet, the summer is not unbearably hot. Spring and fall are delightful and less crowded, but fewer activities are available than in the summer. In winter the South Rim remains open but it can be cold and even snowy; while the North Rim road is open only from the middle of May to mid-October. If you are planning to visit both rims, definitely go in the summer; otherwise any time from April through November will be good.

ADDRESS/TELEPHONE: Superintendent, Grand Canyon National Park, P.O. Box 129, Grand Canyon, AZ 86023. (602) 638-7771. There is prerecorded information available by calling (602) 638-9304.

The North and South rims are two very different worlds. And although they are clearly visible from one another, getting from one to the other is not easy – even if you are not up to taking the two-day trek along the Bright Angel Trail, which connects the two. It is over 200 miles from one rim to the other via SR 64, US 89 and 89A and, finally, SR 67. The drive takes about five hours. That seems incredible when you realize they are only 10 miles apart as the crow flies! Because of the distance involved and the other differences between them, the two rims will be described in separate sections.

The South Rim

Auto Tour/Short Stops

There are approximately 35 miles of good roads on the more heavily visited South Rim which will provide the visitor with several excellent vantage points for seeing the canyon. Soon after passing through the entrance station the road will bring you to **Canyon Village** where most of the visitor facilities are located. From this point the South Rim is divided between the East Rim Drive and West Rim Drive. We'll start with the West Rim, but take note that most of West Rim Drive is closed to private cars during the summer season. But there is a free shuttle bus that travels along its entire length and you can get on and off at any of numerous designated stops. Perhaps the shuttle is even better than your own car because it allows you to take your eyes off the road and concentrate on the scenery. Service is frequent and stops are closely spaced. There is also a shuttle bus that serves only the village area.

Before embarking on the West Rim Drive, stop at the visitor center, where excellent exhibits on the park can be found; you can also pick up information on activities that are taking place there and in the nearby amphitheater.

Several hotels are at the beginning of the West Rim Drive and a canyon rim trail connects them with the visitor center. As this will probably be your first look into and across the canyon, take some time to let its impact really sink in.

I won't attempt to tell you about a best viewing spot, because there is none: wherever you are on the West Rim Drive is outstanding. Traveling from east to west, be sure to stop at **Trailview Overlook, Maricopa Point, the Powell Memorial** (where there is a monument to explorer John Powell), **Hopi Point, Mojave Point, The Abyss, Pima Point,** and **Hermits Rest** at the western terminus of the road. Each of these eight view points will, because of the varying width of the canyon, the angle of view, elevation, and angle of the sun, be quite different from the preceding one. The more views you can take in the better, and all of them are within just a few steps of the roadside parking area or shuttle bus stop.

Now head back to Canyon Village and continue eastbound on the East Rim Drive. Here you will find equally beautiful but different panoramas unfolding before you. The most significant view stops are, in the order you will reach them, **Yavapai Point** (here you should also visit the excellent museum on the culture of local Indian tribes), **Mather Point, Yaki Point, Grandview Point, Moran Point,** and **Lipan Point.** After these six stops there is one final and very different one: **Desert View.** Here you will face an outstanding vista of the Painted Desert, which is the park's eastern neighbor.

From Desert View, continue on out of the park if you are going to be heading for the North Rim or other points east. Otherwise, turn around and head back to Canyon Village. The South Rim tour should take you about five hours.

Getting Out/Longer Stops

While there are several trails that descend into the canyon, including the previously mentioned **Bright Angel Trail** that actually crosses the canyon floor, be aware (perhaps forewarned is a better term), that the climb back up is difficult and should not be attempted unless you are in the best of condition. These trails require an absolute minimum of several hours each. An easier alternative is to walk along the canyon rim. This is especially rewarding along the West Rim during summer, because you won't have to walk back to the same place you started from to get to your car – the shuttle bus will be there whenever you decide that you have had enough walking.

Special Activities

A **horseback ride** along the canyon rim can be arranged in Canyon Village ($). These trips last from one hour to a half-day. **Muleback trips** into the canyon itself are a famous way to see its wonders up close. Some trips are a full day while others are overnight. Although they are certainly not as difficult as hiking into the canyon, they do require a degree of fitness. Also, certain weight restrictions apply for the benefit of the mules! Trips leave from the Canyon Village ($).

Flight-seeing at the Grand Canyon has become very popular ($). Flights are expensive but do add an interesting dimension to your visit. Several different operators offer flights of varying duration. Most are based in the small town of Tusayen, just south of the park entrance.

Another way to see the South Rim is via the **Grand Canyon Railway**, based in the town of Williams. You board a refurbished early 20th-century steam train for the 110-mile round-trip from the depot to the park. It leaves at 9:30 and returns at 5:30, but you spend 4½ hours on the train passing through so-so scenery and only 3½ hours at the South Rim. For a fee in excess of $50, we don't consider it very worthwhile.

Finally, a large-screen **IMAX** film presentation about the Grand Canyon can be seen just south of the entrance station to the park. This is not run by the Park Service or official concessionaire but it is, nevertheless, a worthwhile attraction, especially for the evening if you are staying overnight in the area ($). There is a less expensive film of a similar nature in the village at the **Over The Edge Theater**.

Accommodations

There are several good places to stay on the South Rim. These include the historic **El Tovar Hotel**, with 65 rooms (E), the **Kachina Lodge** with 46 remodeled motel-type units (E), both in the village area. Both the **Maswik Lodge** (285 units ranging from cabins to motel rooms, B to E) and the 50-room **Thunderbird Lodge** (motel accommodations, M) are in the village are, too. The famous **Yavapai Lodge** is near the visitor center. It has 351 rooms (M to E). About eight miles south of the village at the entrance to the park, there are a number of motels in various price ranges. All South Rim in-park accommodation reservations are handled by the Grand Canyon National Park Lodges. Their number is (602) 638-2401 or 638-2631.

Dining

The **El Tovar Hotel** has only a full-service restaurant on the premises. There are large cafeterias in the **Maswik Lodge** and in the **Yavapai Lodge**.

Where Do We Go From Here?

The South Rim of the Grand Canyon is included in *Trip 6*, with or without the option of going on to the North Rim. **Petrified Forest National Park** is only a few hours to the east. Going in the other direction, a very popular destination after visiting the Grand Canyon is **Las Vegas**.

The North Rim

Auto Tour/Short Stops

From the entrance station there are about 22 miles of paved road on the North Rim. Far less crowded than the South Rim, and with fewer facilities, the North Rim is just as beautiful. As a matter of fact, there is an ongoing argument among visitors as to which is more beautiful or more spectacular. There are, fortunately, no losers in this argument – you will love the experience whichever one you see. One thing you won't see here are big crowds – only 10% of Grand Canyon visitors go to the North Rim.

Being higher, the North Rim is cooler and you tend to look down as you look across to the south. There is a small visitor center as you enter this section of the park. The main observation points where you should stop on this drive are **Bright Angel Point, Point Imperial** (located on a side road), **Vista Encantadora, Angel's Window,** and **Cape Royal,** at the very end of the road. As on the South Rim, all of the observation areas are close to the road, so there is relatively little walking. You can complete this shorter road network in just over two hours.

Getting Out/Longer Stops

The same restrictions mentioned about going into the canyon on the south side also apply here. Again, there are really no long trails on the rim itself, but you can walk along it instead of riding. The difference is that there is no shuttle here to pick you up if you get tired.

Accommodations

The only lodging on the North Rim is the **Grand Canyon Lodge,** which has cabins, cottages and motel rooms among its 202 units (M). The facilities here are, especially in the cottages, far more rustic than on the South Rim. Reservations are through TW Recreational Services, (801) 586-7686. The town of Jacob Lake, 44 miles north of the park, has cottages and motel units as well. Grand Canyon Lodge is the focal point for most activities on the North Rim.

Dining

The Grand Canyon Lodge has both a full-service restaurant and a cafeteria.

Where Do We Go From Here?

Again, the North Rim is an option on *Trip 6*. If you are doing both rims, then your visit will, by geographic necessity, take in more of the Arizona attractions included in that suggested routing. If you are doing only the North Rim, then it would be best to combine it with the nearby Utah national parks of **Bryce** and **Zion**. These are easily covered in a loop originating in Las Vegas.

17

Grand Teton National Park

No matter how many national parks you have seen, Grand Teton will almost surely rank up there with the most beautiful. It simply offers some of the best mountain scenery anywhere in the world. In fact, it is quite different from most of the other mountain-dominated national parks in this country, such as Glacier, Mount Rainier or Rocky Mountain. Grand Teton, with its sharp, jagged peaks, seems like a bit of Switzerland in North America.

The highest mountain in the park, at 13,770 feet, is Grand Teton itself. But there are 10 other peaks that reach the impressive height of more than 11,000 feet. The mountains appear even larger than the numbers indicate because all rise abruptly from the otherwise flat terrain of the Jackson Hole Valley.

Despite the emphasis on the beauty of these peaks, Grand Teton is much more than just mountains. With several major lakes, glaciers, forests and the beautiful valley of Jackson Hole, along with the famous Snake River, it is an outdoor enthusiast's playground and a delight to all who visit.

Facts & Figures

LOCATION/GATEWAYS/GETTING THERE: In northwestern Wyoming (almost immediately south of Yellowstone National Park), Grand Teton is accessible from the south via US 191/189, from the north by US 191/287/89 (the Rockefeller Parkway which connects it with Yellowstone), and from the east by US 26/287. The town of Jackson is a few miles south of the park and is the hub for all activity in this area. There is air service into Jackson from a number of larger western cities, but the nearest major one is Salt Lake City. From there, I-15, US 26 and US 189 will take you to Grand Teton, a distance of about 300 miles on good roads that pass through scenic countryside.

YEAR ESTABLISHED: Grand Teton was photographed as early as 1872, and became a national park in 1929.

SIZE: 310,528 acres (or 485 square miles).

ADMISSION FEE: $10, which also entitles you to admission at Yellowstone.

CLIMATE/WHEN TO GO: The park is open all year but snow is heavy in winter and it is very cold. (There is good skiing at nearby resorts.) Summer is generally delightful. A light jacket or sweater is in order for the very cool mornings and evenings, even during the middle of the summer. Rain is rare during this time.

ADDRESS/TELEPHONE: Superintendent, Grand Teton National Park, P.O. Drawer 170, Moose, WY 83012. (307) 739-3300.

Auto Tour/Short Stops

As big as the Grand Teton peaks are, the best way to see the park is not by car. Other methods will be described below, but here is a brief discussion of what can be seen from your car and with a little walking. We describe attractions from south to north as most people enter from that direction (nearest to Jackson) unless they are coming directly from Yellowstone National Park.

Before actually entering Grand Teton, you should make a short side trip (16 miles round-trip) to the **Gros Ventre Slide** area, following directional signs. Although technically within the confines of the **Bridger-Teton National Forest**, this attraction is more commonly associated with Grand Teton. In 1925 a water, mud and rock slide destroyed the town of Kelly. There is still evidence of the slide today on the mountain slope, where a section of the forested slope appears to be "missing." Debris is scattered along the short trail that leads from the parking area.

Grand Teton National Park

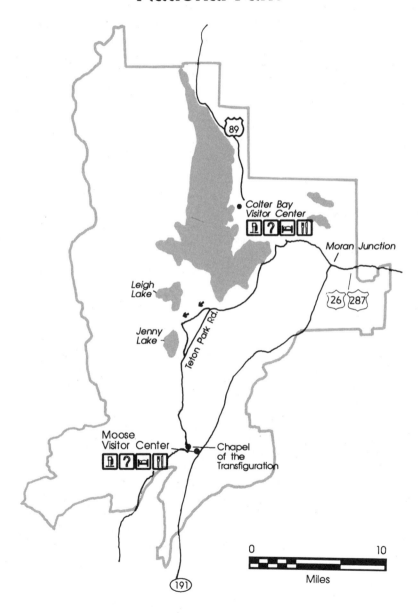

In Grand Teton National Park itself you will, shortly after entering, reach the **Moose Visitor Center**, with exhibits on the park and information on the various activities available. Do take the time to schedule some of the activities that will be described later on. From Moose there are two roads that head north: the Teton Park Road, which is nearer to the mountain range, and the Rockefeller Parkway, which more or less parallels the Snake River. The two link up at the Jackson Lake Lodge. While both afford truly magnificent views, with numerous turnouts where you can admire the mountains, the Teton Park Road is the more scenic. Both roads are very flat and easy to drive, since they run through the valley. Most likely you will be returning to the Jackson town site for some sightseeing there, so you may very well have the opportunity to drive both routes, as the distances within the park along these roads are not great.

One of the most popular sights along the Teton Park Road is the **Chapel of the Transfiguration**. This small log structure was built in 1925 and has a large picture window behind the altar framing a breathtaking mountain view – God's country at its very best. Besides passing numerous mountain and glacier views, the Teton Park Road also goes by **Jenny** and **Jackson Lakes**. Finally, there is a five-mile unpaved spur road to the top of 7,730-foot **Signal Mountain**, which provides an unparalleled view of the entire Teton range, 40 miles long and 20 miles wide.

Driving time up and back in the park, including view stops, should be under four hours.

Getting Out/Longer Stops

Although the scenery from the car and turnouts is extraordinarily beautiful, the real opportunities for enjoying what Grand Teton has to offer are not from behind the driver's seat. So, get off your rear, get out and forget your car!

Mountain climbing is especially popular in Grand Teton. Many of the trails in the park lead up towards the peaks and take from two hours to a full day in walking or hiking time.

At South Jenny Lake Junction take the launch to the west shore of Jenny Lake. Not only will you be in the middle of this beautiful lake and mountain setting but, once on the west side, you will find there is a relatively easy trail leading to **Hidden Falls**. As the trail winds through lush forest and rock coves at the base of precipitous peaks, you will hear the thunder of the falls, but you won't see them until you are practically there. The round-trip walk is just over a half-hour. The Park Service launch operates frequently.

The Colter Bay Nature Trail is a pleasant two-mile stroll through a sub-alpine flower meadow with a magnificent mountain backdrop. **Jackson Lake Lodge** is worth a visit even if you are not going to be staying there. The beautiful timber structure has giant picture windows in its large lobby and lounge which provide a luxurious and comfortable place to ponder the mountains.

Special Activities

One of the most popular ways to see the park is to take a **float trip** on the Snake River ($). Various concessionaires offer trips from five to 20 miles in length (about one to four hours) from several different locations within the park. You can get information from any visitor center, but it is a better idea to make advance reservations. No matter which one you take, the scenery will be spectacular and the stillness on the river a stark contrast to the constant hum of activity on the roadways. These are not whitewater trips (although other portions of the Snake River are among the wildest in the country). The trips, however, use the same type of inflatable rafts that are used on the more adventurous whitewater trips.

Another possibility is the 1½-hour **cruise** on Jackson Lake ($). Although the launch trip on Jenny Lake is not a cruise in the same sense, it does give you glimpses of similar scenery. Therefore, if time is a problem, I would choose the Snake River float trip and the Jenny Lake launch rather than the Jackson Lake cruise. If you have plenty of time, all are worthwhile.

Horse and wagon rides ranging from two hours to a half-day are also available ($); inquire at the visitor center for further information.

The **Colter Bay Visitor Center** in the northern portion of the park offers exhibits on the culture of the native Indian tribes in the area. If you happen to be in the park on a Friday evening, consider the **Laubin Ancient Indian Dances**, performed at Jackson Lake Lodge at 8:30 p.m.

One last item. Twelve miles northwest of the town of Jackson is the **Jackson Hole Aerial Tram**. This is a 2½-mile excursion to the top of 10,450-foot Rendezvous Mountain. Although not in the park itself, the views of the entire Teton Range as well as the valley are nothing short of spectacular ($).

Accommodations

Lodging within the park boundaries ranges from the luxurious **Jackson Lake Lodge**, with 385 motor-inn type rooms (E), to the log cabins of **Jenny Lake Lodge**, with 30 units (E). At the **Colter Bay Village** there are 167 cabins (M), and the **Signal Mountain Lodge** also has cottages. There are 79 rooms in this facility (M to E). Finally, the **Togwotes Mountain Lodge** is a small establishment with 28 nice rooms (E). If you are not going to stay in the park, you will then be staying overnight in Jackson, which offers over three dozen hotels to choose from. All in-park reservations (except Signal Mountain) are through the Grand Teton Lodge Company, (800) 628-9988.

Dining

Both the **Mural Room** (in Jackson Lake Lodge) and the **Aspens Restaurant** (in Signal Mountain Lodge) have first-class, full-service restaurants as well as coffee shops. The **Colter Bay Village** also has these amenities. The **Jenny Lake Lodge** and the **Togwotes Mountain Lodge** both have restaurants. A large variety of places to eat, including all of the fast food chains, are available in Jackson.

Where Do We Go From Here?

Suggested Trip 5 is an excellent scenic drive, but if time is short you should at least see **Grand Teton National Park** and its northern neighbor, **Yellowstone National Park**. The two are only a half-hour (but a world) apart! Together they provide so much to see and do that they are a major vacation trip all by themselves. They can also be covered in a loop from Salt Lake City, which itself has many points of interest.

18

Great Smoky Mountains National Park

This park is close to major population centers, but its lush greenery and pleasantly rounded peaks create a soothing aura of tranquillity. And, of course, there is the famous "smoke" that seems to perpetually hang over it. Actually, this bluish haze is the condensation of vapors from the thick vegetation. Even on the sunniest days you will probably see the haze which gives the park, and the Blue Ridge Mountains of which it is a part, their name.

Most of the park is at an altitude of 5,000-6,000 feet and there are about 20 peaks over 6,000 feet, making this one of the highest tracts of land in the east. The variety of plants and flowers that cover the mountains is extraordinary; few are without this cover and those are called, appropriately, "balds."

Facts & Figures

LOCATION/GATEWAYS/GETTING THERE: Its area about evenly divided between Tennessee and North Carolina, the park sits astride US 441 between Knoxville, Tennessee and Asheville, North Carolina. Knoxville is the larger of the two cities and, therefore, the best gateway. The southern terminus of the Blue Ridge Parkway at Cherokee runs directly into the south entrance of the park.

YEAR ESTABLISHED: The park opened in 1926 but was not officially dedicated until 14 years later. It took that long to buy up all of the land, which previously had been in private hands. Even today there are clusters of private land within the park. Please respect such private property if you come upon it.

SIZE: 520,269 acres (or 813 square miles).

ADMISSION FEE: None.

CLIMATE/WHEN TO GO: The weather is delightful in spring and fall and even summer is not uncomfortable because of the elevation. Although the park is open all year, the period from November through April is not the best time for a visit – winter can be quite cold and many facilities are not available during this time.

ADDRESS/TELEPHONE: Superintendent, Great Smoky Mountains National Park, 107 Park Headquarters Road, Gatlinburg, TN 37738. (615) 436-1200. For information on the Blue Ridge Parkway, contact: Blue Ridge Parkway Headquarters, 200 BB&T Building, 1 Pack Square, Asheville NC 28801. (904) 259-0701.

Auto Tour/Short Stops

The Newfoundland Gap Road (US 441) traverses the width of the park for 33 miles from Gatlinburg to Cherokee. However, there are 170 miles of other paved roads, some of which will bring you into areas of the park that should be seen in a comprehensive visit. The suggested route will begin at the northern entrance. If you are coming from the other direction, simply reverse the entire route.

At the park entrance look for the beginning of the **Roaring Fork Motor Nature Trail**. The unique one-way route covers six miles in an area that is particularly blessed with a variety of flora. There are more than 1,500 different plant varieties within Great Smoky Mountains. Returning to the main road you will soon arrive at the **Sugarlands Visitor Center**, where there are excellent exhibits about the park's history, animal and plant life, and local culture.

Just beyond the visitor center, turn off US 441 onto the Little River Road. This will be the beginning of a 60-mile round-trip leading through the **Cade's Cove** section of the park. Besides being one of the park's most scenic areas, a one-way loop road at Cade's Cove

Great Smoky Mountains National Park

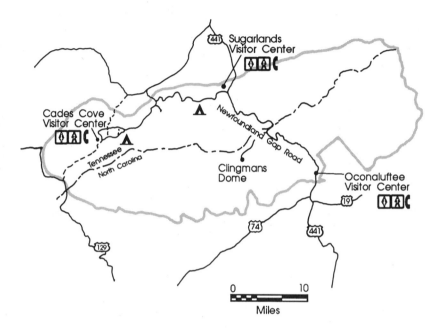

passes through a recreated 19th-century agricultural community. A visitor center here is devoted to the surrounding historical village.

Returning to the main road we are now finally ready to embark on the first half of the Newfoundland Gap Road. There are frequent overlooks as the road climbs to its high point and you should definitely stop to take a better look at the **Chimney Tops** and **Mount Le Conte** pullouts. Soon you will arrive at **Newfoundland Gap** itself, the half-way point of the road. It is also the border between Tennessee and North Carolina as well as the junction for the road to **Clingman's Dome** (closed in winter). This route is seven miles each way and ends just a half-mile short of Clingman's Dome which, at 6,643 feet, is the highest point in the park and in the state of Tennessee. (See next section for trail description.)

Now you can head back to the main highway and continue on, negotiating some gentle switchbacks as you descend to the **Ocon-**

aluftee Visitor Center at the southern end of the park. The **Pioneer Farmstead**, a living museum, is of interest here.

The route just described covers almost 120 miles and, with the stops mentioned, will take about five hours.

Getting Out/Longer Stops

There are hundreds of miles of trails in the park, virtually all of which would have to be considered back-country hiking trails. There are two shorter trails that are worth mentioning. The first is on the nature motor loop mentioned previously. A trail leads to the very attractive **Grotto Falls**, and takes about 40 minutes. The second is more of a must. This is the half-mile trail leading to the observation tower at the top of Clingman's Dome. Not only is the view more splendid than most other vistas in the park, but you will be able to tell your friends that you literally climbed to the top of the Smokies! Allow one hour for the complete trip, which isn't that long but is steep in places.

Special Activities

The previously mentioned Cade's Cove and Pioneer Farmstead have frequent **craft demonstrations** and other activities. Also, for those who want to take a break from driving their own cars, **bus tours** of the park are available from Gatlinburg ($). These trips will not cover as much ground as you would on your own, but the informed commentary is interesting. But keep in mind that, if you will be continuing your trip in the opposite direction from Gatlinburg, you will have to drive through the park on your own in any event.

Accommodations & Dining

There are no adequate overnight lodging facilities within the park itself (the only in-park lodging being the LeConte Lodge, which is only accessible via several miles of hiking), but there is a wide choice at either end, especially in Gatlinburg, a major resort area. Here you will find everything from modest budget motels to fully-equipped luxury resorts. Many have a panoramic view of the surrounding area. For full meals you will also have to wait until you are in Gatlinburg or Cherokee, but light meals and snacks are available in several areas of the park, including Cade's Cove and Sugarlands.

Where Do We Go From Here?

The logical extensions to this park are the **Blue Ridge Parkway** and **Shenandoah**, both a part of *Suggested Trip 1*. For a shorter vacation, the many attractions in the park and nearby at Gatlinburg and Asheville can provide a compact but enjoyable trip.

19

Haleakala National Park

Haleakala, or "House of the Sun," is the crater of a dormant Hawaiian volcano (the last eruption was in 1790). It is one of the largest such craters in the world, measuring 7½ by 2½ miles, and more than 3,000 feet deep from the rim of the crater to its deepest recesses.

The many colors within the crater are highly unusual in a volcanic formation. There are cinder cones throughout the crater which give the appearance of a miniature mountain range. Other sections look like a desert. This, and the lack of vegetation in most parts of the crater, give it a moon-like appearance. Visibility within the crater varies greatly, practically from one minute to the next. Even on the sunniest days there are times when clouds will suddenly appear overhead and seem to become "stuck" in the crater. But wait a bit and they are likely to lift away, revealing the panoramic crater vista. It's an astonishing sight when cloud-filled, as well, and can easily transport you onto another planet, if only for a moment! Vistas of the ocean and of the island of Maui below are also unforgettable from the House of the Sun.

Facts & Figures

LOCATION/GATEWAYS/GETTING THERE: In the eastern portion of the island of Maui, the park is about 27 miles from the airport and town center of Kahului. It is, of course, just a short flight from Honolulu, if you are making your base there. From Kahului follow SRs 36, 37, 377 and 378 in that sequence to reach Haleakala.

YEAR ESTABLISHED: A part of the national park system since 1916 (as a section of Hawaii Volcanoes National Park), Haleakala was established as a separate national park in 1960.

SIZE: 28,655 acres (or 45 square miles).

ADMISSION FEE: $4.

CLIMATE/WHEN TO GO: Although any time of the year is the right time to visit Hawaii in general, keep in mind that at the top of the crater it can be as much as 30° cooler than at sea level. So bring along a jacket, even if you are going to be in a bathing suit later in the day. If you are here in January or February you might even encounter a bit of snow. Morning, which is generally sunny, is the best time to visit the park throughout the year. For those willing to arise in the middle of the night, sunrise at Haleakala Crater is considered by many to be one of the most beautiful sights anywhere in the world!

ADDRESS/TELEPHONE: Superintendent, Haleakala National Park, Box 369, Makawao, Maui, HI 96768. (808) 572-9306.

Auto Tour/Short Stops

In the 27 miles from Kahului to the park you will climb from just above sea level to over 7,000 feet. Most of this climb takes place during the second half of the trip. The road twists and turns constantly; with many switchbacks and steep grades. But the drive is not as difficult as you might expect. Still, keep your eyes on the road – there will be plenty of time for seeing the sights once you get there.

Just inside the entrance station, turn into the **Hosmer Grove**. Here, a quarter-mile nature trail has exotic plants and explains the relationship of these plants to the surroundings. Note that the Silversword plant grows only at Haleakala. It can be seen in several parts of the park. Within the park itself, the road continues to climb until it reaches the summit of Puu Ulaula at 10,023 feet. Before getting there, however, there are two outstanding overlooks. The first is **Leleiwi Overlook**. There is a good view of the crater from here. More significantly, if the cloud conditions are just right, your shadow will be projected onto the clouds in the crater. Rainbows are also frequently seen from this vantage point.

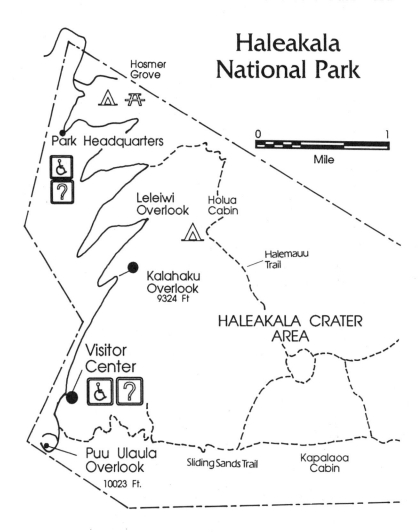

Haleakala National Park

A bit further up the road is **Kalahaku Overlook**, with a panoramic view of the crater and many of its cinder cones. Then comes the Visitor Center where there are numerous exhibits on the crater and the environment of Haleakala. Beyond the center is the summit of **Puu Ulaula**, which not only provides vistas of the crater but equally dramatic views of the ocean and the valley of the isle of Maui far below. The road ends at the summit.

You should allocate half a day to see the main section of the park, including the round-trip drive from Kahului.

Ohe'o Gulch

This easternmost section of the park slopes downward to the ocean. In Ohe'o Gulch you can see a fine example of a rain forest, several scenic pools and beautiful waterfalls. Unfortunately, the park road to the House of the Sun's crater does not connect with this section. To get there from Kahului or from the main portion of the park, it is a 70-mile drive each way (via SRs 36, 360 and 31) on the Hana Road. It has breathtaking vistas of the ocean and mountains, but it is not the best road in the world, with over 600 turns along its length. Although Ohe'o Gulch is quite pretty, it may be anticlimactic after the panorama seen along the Hana Road – surely one of the world's most beautiful drives. Review a Hawaii guidebook (or see *Suggested Trip 11)* to determine whether the other attractions on the Hana Road are of interest to you. If they are, then by all means see the Ohe'o Gulch as well. Allow a full day for the complete round-trip to Hana and the Gulch, including sightseeing.

Getting Out/Longer Stops

Back to the crater area for a few moments now. While most of the park's trails go into the crater and are long and difficult for the casual visitor, there is one trail that you should definitely consider. **The White Hill Trail**, near the visitor center, is just over a quarter-mile long. It is fairly steep and you should allow about 45 minutes to accomplish it. It provides some exceptional views that nicely juxtapose the barren crater with the color surrounding it.

Special Activities

For those who don't want to leave Haleakala without having ventured into the crater but feel they won't be able to climb back out, there are guided **horseback tours** available ($). In addition, if you are apprehensive about the nature of the road to and from the top, Gray Line of Hawaii does provide numerous half- and full-day **bus tours** ($) that include Haleakala National Park, but remember that you will see much more on your own.

Accommodations & Dining

There are no lodgings or restaurants in the park. However, since you will see the crater in a half-day, Maui's many resort areas are within easy driving distance. Some restaurants are considerably closer, along the route back to Kahului. If you are going to the Ohe'o Gulch, there are several towns along the Hana Road that have restaurants of all types. Some towns also have lodging, but not the variety or luxury found in the western part of the island.

Where Do We Go From Here?

Obviously, any trip to Haleakala will be a part of a larger Hawaiian vacation. *Suggested Trip 11* provides many ideas for developing a Hawaiian itinerary.

20

Hawaii Volcanoes National Park

This is nature's workshop – probably among the most active volcanic areas in the world. Here you will not find the explosive, highly destructive type of volcano, but a more gently flowing lava that slowly builds up into relatively shallow craters known as calderas. Because of the type of volcanic activity here, Hawaii Volcanoes National Park has sometimes been referred to as the "Drive-In Volcano." But don't let that nickname fool you. Its power is still awesome and there are occasions where sections of the park must be closed because of recurring volcanic activity. Some local residents can tell you how this "gentle" volcano has swallowed up their homes. If an area has temporarily been declared off limits, do not attempt to circumvent that limitation – it is for your own safety.

Most likely on your visit you will see only steam escaping from vents in the crater and, of course, evidence of past eruptions. But that alone is worth the visit, for the park is a highly unusual experience. The crater itself and past lava flows are both educational and impressive. It is a strange, eerie place rather than one of exceptional beauty.

Facts & Figures

LOCATION/GATEWAYS/GETTING THERE: On the Big Island of Hawaii, the park is 30 miles southwest of the island's largest city of Hilo. From the Kailua-Kona resort coast on the western side of the island it is 96 miles. SR 11 provides access to the park from either gateway, both of which have convenient inter-island air service.

YEAR ESTABLISHED: The park was established in 1916.

SIZE: 229,177 acres (or 350 square miles).

ADMISSION FEE: $5.

CLIMATE/WHEN TO GO: Up at the crater rim level the weather is substantially cooler than at sea level. But the park is open all year and is suitable for touring at any time. A sweater or light jacket should be carried at all times, especially for chilly mornings.

ADDRESS/TELEPHONE: Superintendent, Hawaii Volcanoes National Park, Hawaii National Park, HI 96178. (808) 967-7311 is the number for general information; call (808) 967-7977 for up-to-the-minute information on eruptions and road conditions.

Auto Tour/Short Stops

Hawaii Volcanoes National Park has an excellent system of roads that bring you in close proximity to most points of interest, but there are substantial opportunities for more detailed exploration on foot as well.

Note: The information contained herein was correct at press time, but temporary road closures or detours may be necessary on occasion because of recent volcanic activity. This is especially true along the currently more active Chain of Craters Road as it approaches the sea. Call beforehand to check on current road conditions.

Our route assumes you will arrive from Hilo, and go clockwise around the crater. The **Crater Rim Road** encircles **Kilauea Crater** for 11 miles. The crater itself is 2½ miles across and there are many side craters and craters within craters. The road elevation averages 4,000 feet, but it is a good road and getting up to that level from the coast is an easy drive.

Start your tour at the **Kilauea Visitor Center** where you can view several films and exhibits on the park, some of which document past eruptions. There are several trails here that will be discussed in the next section.

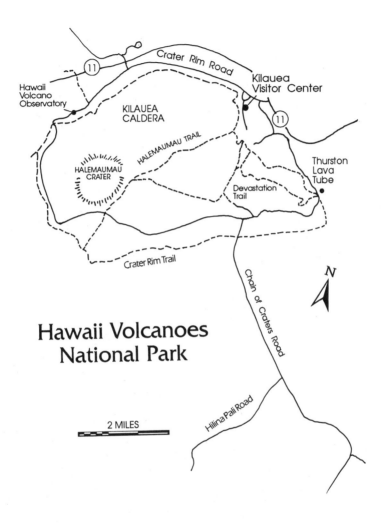

Crater Rim Road

11

Hawaii
Volcano
Observatory

KILAUEA
CALDERA

Kilauea
Visitor Center

11

HALEMAUMAU TRAIL

HALEMAUMAU
CRATER

Thurston
Lava
Tube

Devastation
Trail

Crater Rim Trail

Chain of Craters Road

N

Hawaii Volcanoes National Park

Hilina Pali Road

2 MILES

Beginning the circle tour, you will come to the **Waldron Ledge Overlook** and then an overlook into **Kilauea Iki Crater**, a large side crater created in 1959. Just ahead is the short trail leading to the **Thurston Lava Tube**, a 500-foot tunnel created when the outer portion of a lava flow hardened, allowing lava on the inside to continue flowing out. The trail includes some stairs, but is easy and totals just over a quarter-mile, including the cave-like tunnel of the tube itself.

Less than a mile further on is the parking area for the Devastation Trail, which will be described in the next section. Also near this point is the junction with the Chain of Craters Road, which leaves the rim and extends down to the coastal section of the park. This road, in addition to passing by historic Hawaiian villages and temples, offers views of many small craters and other volcanic formations, including many lava flows. The vista of the Pacific Ocean as you reach the coast is also spectacular. The road used to go out of the park and connect back to Hilo, but lava flows in the 1980's (which continue sporadically today) will likely keep this section of the road closed for several years. Only a few miles along the coast are open. Still, Chain of Craters Road, a round-trip distance of about 50 miles from Crater Rim Drive, is a worthwhile detour. After seeing this area, work your way back to the Crater Rim Road and stop at the **Keanakakoi Crater Overlook.**

After the road crosses a 1982 lava flow you'll come to the parking area for a short (10-minute), easy trail to an overlook facing the **Haleamaumau Crater.** This is one of the largest and most active vents in the Kilauea Caldera. It is one of the eeriest spots in the park, with steam coming from the ground, strange aromas, and a mostly barren, moon-like landscape.

About two miles ahead is the **Hawaii Volcano Observatory.** Although this research institute is closed to the public, you can get a spectacular view of the entire caldera from the adjacent overlook on the **Uwekahuna Bluff**, at an elevation of 4,077 feet (the highest point on the road).

Leave the Crater Rim Road once agai, turning onto the Mauna Loa Road. This road extends for a few miles before ending at the trail head to 13,677-foot **Mauna Loa**, where snow is common in winter. You may not be making this long and difficult climb, but the drive to the road's end is worthwhile because the view of Mauna Loa is excellent from there. Mauna Loa is the world's largest mountain in cubic mass. At a height of 30,000 feet from its base beneath the sea to the summit, it is even higher than Mount Everest. At the beginning of the road, closer to Crater Rim Drive, there are several points of interest. One is the **Tree Molds**, actual trees that were encased in lava. When the interior rotted away, what remained was a "lava tree." The Kipuka Puaulu (Bird Park) trail is here as well and will be described in the next section.

Now return to the Crater Rim Road and you will shortly arrive back at the Kilauea Visitor Center, starting point for several other trails to be described later. Total distance (including the round-trip down the Chain of Craters and Mauna Loa Strip Roads) is 70 miles. With the many view stops and short trails, you should allow about four hours for the Auto Tour.

Getting Out/Longer Stops

The casual visitor is not equipped to deal with the strenuous climb to Mauna Loa; the same is true for many of the trails that lead into and across the Kilauea Caldera. But there are many other trails that are easy and rewarding.

Devastation Trail is one of the most popular in the park. It is about 1¼ miles long and takes a little more than a half-hour one way. There is a parking area at either end, so if one member of your party is willing to skip the trail or to run back and get the car, it is not necessary for everyone to make the return trip. The trail consists of a boardwalk through an area that was completely devastated in an earlier eruption. Over the years, much vegetation has reappeared but it is still a desolate place. The boardwalk has been constructed so that the natural regrowth of the area is not interfered with by visitors; so please, always remain on the boardwalk in this living laboratory.

The next walk of interest is **Kipuka Puaulu (or Bird Park) Trail**. This is a one-mile nature trail and takes about 30 minutes. Many varieties of plants and flowers will be seen on this marked trail.

Finally, two trails that originate at the visitor center are the **Sulfur Banks** and **Sandalwood Trails**. The former is only about a quarter-mile and takes under a half-hour. It passes numerous vents from which yellowish deposits of sulfur have accumulated over the years. The rotten-egg aroma of the sulfur is unmistakable. The other trail is much longer, taking an hour or more, but it hugs the crater and provides excellent views. The two trails cross at one point so that you can combine them on a single walk rather than returning to the visitor center and starting over. The return climb on the Sandalwood Trail is fairly steep in places.

Accommodations

The only lodging within the park is the **Volcano House**, an old and quaint, if not attractive 37-room lodge perched right on the rim of the crater (M). Call (808) 967-7311 for reservations. There is a wide variety of accommodations in Hilo if you finish the park at the end of the day. Even more are in Kona, but that is a much longer drive.

Dining

Volcano House has both a full-service restaurant and a small cafeteria-style shop for quick snacks or lighter meals. Again, you would have to go to Hilo to find a variety of restaurants.

Where Do We Go From Here?

As was the case with visiting Haleakala National Park, anyone coming to Hawaii Volcanoes will certainly be incorporating it into an overall Hawaiian vacation. Once again, you are referred to *Trip 11* for further suggestions on a four-island tour.

21

Lake Mead National Recreation Area

With the completion of Hoover Dam and the resulting creation of Lake Mead and Lake Mojave in the 1930s, the Lake Mead National Recreation Area came into existence in what had previously been a large area of mostly barren desert surrounding the Colorado River with its intermittent flooding and dry periods. Although the primary purpose behind establishment of the recreation area was to provide water sports enthusiasts with myriad outdoor activities, the area contains enough beautiful scenery to merit inclusion in this guide.

Extending for over 115 miles along both sides of the Colorado River on the Arizona and Nevada borders, the area is comprised of Lake Mead, one of the largest man-made lakes in North America, and the smaller Lake Mojave. Surrounding both lakes are colorful mountains, canyons and ravines. The elevation of the area ranges from 517 feet to as much as 6,990 feet, providing a dramatic topographic setting.

Facts & Figures

LOCATION/GATEWAYS/GETTING THERE: In the southern corner of Nevada and northeastern Arizona, the recreation area is under an hour drive from Las Vegas (the primary gateway) via US 93 and is adjacent to the town of Boulder City. It is also accessible via US 93 from Kingman, Arizona and several other points.

YEAR ESTABLISHED: The recreation area was created in 1964.

SIZE: 1,496,601 acres (or 2,338 square miles), an area half the size of Connecticut.

ADMISSION FEE: There is no charge for entering the area.

CLIMATE/WHEN TO GO: Don't let all the water in those vast lakes fool you – this is still the desert, and summertime temperatures reach 100° and higher under a relentless sun, although it is more comfortable when you are out on the water. Winters can be surprisingly chilly, so the best time to visit is either spring or fall.

ADDRESS/TELEPHONE: Headquarters, Lake Mead National Recreation Area, 601 Nevada Highway, Boulder City, NV 89005. (702) 293-8906 or 8907.

Auto Tour/Short Stops

There is an extensive system of roads within the recreation area. Arriving from Las Vegas, stop at the visitor center at the junction of US 93 and Lakeshore Drive to get additional information and see the exhibits. Outside of the center is a botanical garden, which has samples of the flora to be found in the surrounding desert. Then head south on US 93 again. Soon the road will start to twist and climb through the forbidding, dark red mountains and the narrow canyons until you suddenly reach **Hoover Dam**. The sight of the huge structure tucked into this strange landscape is one that most visitors will not soon forget.

Continue down the road, which actually crosses the crest of the dam. Several small museums have information about the dam's construction and functions. There are impressive views of Lake Mead on one side and the canyon of the Colorado River on the other. These can be seen from observation points at each end and from the walkway that runs the entire width of the dam.

You should then continue for about four miles on US 93 into Arizona (the state border being the exact mid-point of the dam) to see some of the beautiful scenery in the **Black Mountains**. The winding road is exciting but still easy to drive. There is a side road (unfortunately, it is unpaved) to Kingman Wash that has a spectacular view of Lake Mead. Then retrace your route to the visitor center.

Lake Mead
National Park

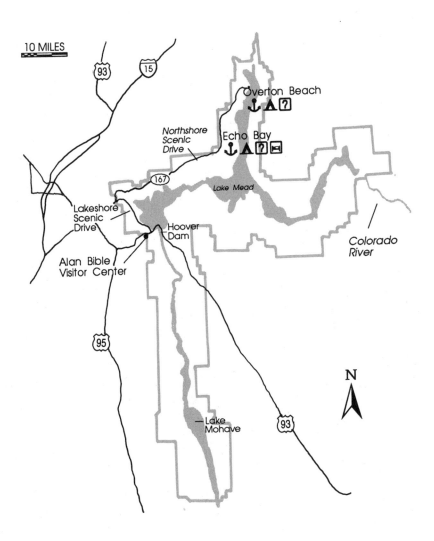

At this point you can go north or south. I strongly suggest that you head north. If you follow the southern route via US 95 the road will take you to **Lake Mojave** and **Davis Dam**, a distance of about 67 miles from the Hoover Dam. However, the area is less developed and the scenery is similar but not as dramatic as on the northern route. Also, if you drive down to Davis Dam, the return route will have to be over the same road – 134 total extra miles. So, spend the time more wisely by heading north via Lakeshore Drive and Northshore Drive. It is 53 miles from the visitor center to Overton Beach. Along the way there are several excellent views of the Black Mountains, Lake Mead and various canyons and coves. At Overton Beach you can avoid back-tracking and return to Las Vegas via the Valley of Fire State Park and I-15. The **Valley of Fire**, adjacent to but not part of the recreation area, is an area of desolate beauty and should be combined with a visit to this part of the Lake Mead area.

The Auto Tour of the Hoover Dam, the visitor center, crossing into Arizona and the north shore route should take you about 3½ hours without the special activities described below. Doing the southern portion of the recreation area would require another three hours and really is not worth the time unless your next destination is in that direction.

Getting Out/Longer Stops

There are many hiking trails that lead from just off the road through the mountains to vistas of the lake and small canyons. However, most are difficult and none should be attempted if you are visiting in the heat of the summer months.

Special Activities

Of course there are many water sports available, including fishing, boating, swimming, water-skiing and diving. There are launching ramps if you bring your own boat. Two of the most popular activities are **tours of Hoover Dam** and **cruises on Lake Mead** ($). The Hoover Dam tour takes about 35 minutes and goes down to the bottom of the dam, where you will learn much about its operation. There is often a long line waiting for the tour, so try to arrive early in the day. The cruise on Lake Mead lasts about 1¼ hours and leaves from the Lake Mead Marina on Lakeshore Drive. It provides a view of the dam from the lake side, which is entirely different from what you see on the road or atop the dam itself. In addition, the mountains and canyons as seen from the lake are quite beautiful and certainly much more colorful than the Black Mountains seen on the Auto Tour. The waters of Lake Mead are an exquisite blue, adding to the beauty of the scene.

Accommodations & Dining

Several towns, including Echo Bay and Boulder City, have overnight accommodations. But even after a full day of sightseeing you have ample time to get back to Las Vegas, with its fantastic variety of accommodations, that is what I suggest you plan for. Probably the only meal you will need to have at the recreation area is lunch. Several modest places are available near the various marinas and full-service restaurants can be found in both Boulder City and Echo Bay.

Where Do We Go From Here?

Lake Mead is part of the extensive itinerary in *Trip 7*. A shorter alternative is to include Lake Mead with a tour from Las Vegas covering **Bryce**, **Zion** and the North Rim of the **Grand Canyon**. If visiting in winter, another possible alternative (if Las Vegas is your base) is to visit **Death Valley**; but plan any visit there very carefully. Death Valley generally requires at least two days from Las Vegas with an overnight stay in the valley itself. Its great scenery is truly rewarding but has not been included in this book because of its great distance from other attractions and the harsh environment which, for practical purposes, limits the visiting season to the period from October through March.

22

Lassen Volcanic National Park

The nation's first volcanic national park, Lassen contains not only the dormant 10,457-foot Lassen Peak, but three other major volcanic structures – two shield volcanoes and a cinder cone, ranging from 6,000 to 8,000 feet. Virtually every other type of volcanic activity is also present here, including lava flows, hot springs, mudpots and boiling lakes.

Lassen's last big eruption occurred from 1914-1915, although major steam eruptions continued all the way through 1921 and, even today, still occur periodically. Scientists are convinced that we haven't heard the last from Lassen! However, for the time being you can visit without fear of any dangerous activity from the mountain. You will find that Lassen is much more than the remains of a volcanic eruption. It contains many beautiful mountain vistas and dozens of tranquil lakes for you to enjoy. For winter sports enthusiasts there is even excellent skiing available.

Facts & Figures

LOCATION/GATEWAYS/GETTING THERE: In north-central California, Lassen Park is 47 miles off I-5 at Redding, via SR 44, or 46 miles via SR 36 from the Red Bluff exit of I-5. It is about 235 miles northeast of San Francisco via I-80, I-505 and I-5 to either of the above access routes.

YEAR ESTABLISHED: The park was established in 1916, right after the conclusion of the most recent major eruptive period.

SIZE: 106,372 acres (or 166 square miles).

ADMISSION FEE: $5.

CLIMATE/WHEN TO GO: Even though the park is open all year, winter snows close some roads. From the middle of June through mid- to late October is the primary touring season. It is very warm but not nearly so hot as the surrounding valleys because of the park's high elevation.

ADDRESS/TELEPHONE: Superintendent, Lassen Volcanic National Park, 38050 Highway 36 East, Mineral, CA 96063. (916) 595-4444.

Auto Tour/Short Stops

The Lassen Park Road extends for about 30 miles from the northwest entrance at Manzanita to the southwest entrance just north of Mineral. Along its route are many of the major points of interest in the park. Unfortunately, most of the largest lakes are in the eastern portion of the park, to which there is no road access. Even so, there is much to see on the Auto Tour. We will begin our trip from the northernmost entrance, but you can easily reverse the entire route if it suits you better.

Just inside the entrance station is a small visitor center where you can get information and view exhibits about the park. **Manzanita Lake** is a beautiful blue jewel nestled in the mountains. Although there is no roadside stopping point you can pull off the main road and into the adjacent campground for a closer look. The road then passes through an area called the **Chaos Crags** (to the driver's left) and **Chaos Jumbles** (to the right). The Crags are large plugs of lava strewn about on the mountainside, as if by some giant. Also here is the **Dwarf Forest**, so-called because of the small coniferous trees in this area. They are not young trees, as many visitors mistakenly assume, but full-grown specimens, some over 300 years old. The Jumbles are, in a geological sense, the same formations as the Crags but numerous rock slides have scattered them about, mostly at lower elevations than the Crags.

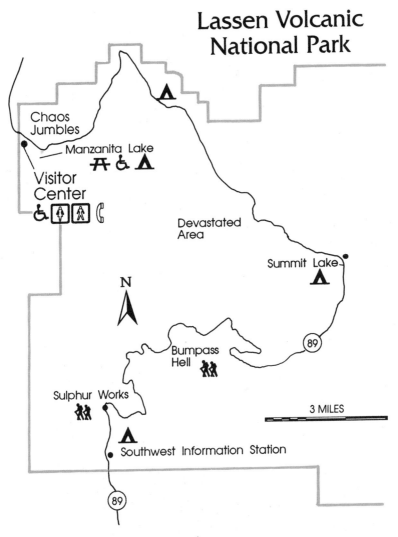

Lassen Volcanic National Park

A bit beyond this area is a roadside pullout by a formation known as the **Hot Rock**, a large volcanic boulder weighing several hundred tons, although it doesn't look as if it would weigh that much. Go ahead and try to move it, as hundreds of thousands of others have, without any success. You will now be entering the **Devastated Area**. The passage of almost 80 years has restored much of the landscape. In fact, the forest has regrown nicely, but there are still piles of rocks and volcanic debris clearly in evidence from two nearby viewing overlooks – **Emigrant Pass** and Hat Lake. The next two scenic panoramas of mountains, both near and distant, are at

Summit Lake and **Lupine**. Later, you will pass **Diamond Peak**, where there is sometimes steam pouring out from vents in the mountainside. There is no place to stop here, but right after Diamond Peak you can park your car at the **Sulphur Works Thermal Area**. Here a short boardwalk trail leads past a number of thermal spots. The yellowish color and awful aroma of sulphur are prominent in this 15-minute loop walk. More thermal activity is in Bumpass Hell (see next section).

After you have toured the thermal areas, you will reach the ski chalet which, of course, is mostly inactive during the summer season. Beyond this is the southwest entrance station, where there is another small visitor center.

You should plan on spending a bit more than two hours on the Auto Tour.

Getting Out/Longer Stops

The back-country trails as well as those to the higher summits are long and strenuous. There are two significant hikes that are much easier and that you should definitely consider. The first is at **Kings Creek Meadows**, where a 1¼-mile trail leads to beautiful Kings Creek Falls. There are some fairly steep grades, but the trail is not terribly difficult and can be done, round-trip, in about 1½ hours.

The second and perhaps more important trail is the **Bumpass Hell Trail**. This one-mile trail leads to Bumpass Hell, the primary area of thermal activity in the park. While not nearly as large or as spectacular as those found in Yellowstone, the trail will still take you past many boiling pots, mudpots, hot springs and other volcanic activity. Allow two hours for the complete trip.

Accommodations & Dining

Finding a good place to stay may be the most difficult part of a visit to Lassen. The only place in the park is the small **Drakesbad Guest Ranch** (E). But this is not on the main route – you have to exit the southwest corner of the park and take SR 89 to Chester Warner Valley Road, re-enter the park and continue along this partially unpaved route. The total distance from the southwest entrance station is 42 miles. These accommodations are quite modest, but are in the heart of the back-country, with an absolutely beautiful mountain setting and many guest activities, such as horseback riding.

There are plenty of motels in either Red Bluff or Redding, although these are a fair distance from the park. If you intend to head east after the park the distance is even greater, since Susanville, where there is a good choice of lodging, is about 70 miles away. I suggest you plan to arrive at Lassen early in the day so that you have time for all the sightseeing but can still get back to a place where lodging is available.

The same problem occurs with dining options. At the ski chalet just north of the Mineral entrance, however, you can at least have a snack or light lunch, so you won't starve.

Where Do We Go From Here?

The suggested trip which includes Lassen is more associated with the many sights of Oregon (*Trip 9*). If that itinerary is not to your liking, an alternative is to use San Francisco as your base and see **Lassen, Yosemite** and the **Whiskeytown-Shasta-Trinity National Recreation Area**. The northern California coast and Redwood country is also within range of a trip including Lassen as its prime destination. For a trip originating in San Francisco you have the option of ending up in Reno (and Lake Tahoe) instead of returning to San Francisco.

23

Mammoth Cave National Park

This is probably the largest system of caves in the world, but not all of it has been discovered yet. At the present time, there are over 300 miles of mapped passageways on five different levels, which does make it the largest known cave.

The cave and its colorful formations are the result of water seeping through the limestone rock above. While there are some caverns whose formations might be more delicate or beautiful than at Mammoth, no other cave can offer the sheer variety of sights to be seen here. Its size alone is awesome enough, and some rooms are so large that you will barely feel that you are inside a cave at all. Although evidence of human habitation in the cave goes back 4,000 years, white settlers discovered it only in 1798. Its huge deposits of saltpeter provided over 200 tons of gunpowder, primarily during the War of 1812. A fascinating world in itself, Mammoth Cave and the attractive surrounding areas that have been set aside as national park lands are certainly ingredients for a trip to remember.

Facts & Figures

LOCATION/GATEWAYS/GETTING THERE: Not far from Blue Grass Country, Mammoth Cave is off I-65 via SR 70 in south-central Kentucky. Use the Cave City exit. It is just northeast of the larger town of Bowling Green. The major gateways are Nashville, approximately 1½ hours south via I-65, and Louisville, about 1¾ hours north, also by I-65.

YEAR ESTABLISHED: Though the cave's existence has been known for centuries, it became a national park in 1926.

SIZE: 52,390 acres (or 82 square miles).

ADMISSION FEES: There is no fee on admission to the park, but all cave tours are on a fee basis, beginning at $5. Information and reservations are available from MISTIX. See "For More Information" section at the back of this book.

CLIMATE/WHEN TO GO: The park is open all year and the cave itself has a constant temperature of 54°F, so a sweater or jacket is prudent at all times. This area of Kentucky is hot and humid in summer and fairly brisk in winter. The fall and spring are delightful; as a matter of fact the fall foliage, though not on the level of New England's famous colors, is quite beautiful. Most park activities are available from April through October, so those are the best times for a visit.

ADDRESS/TELEPHONE: Superintendent, Mammoth Cave National Park, Mammoth Cave, KY 42259. (502) 758-2251 for general information. For cave information call (502) 758 2328.

Auto Tour/Getting Out

There are only a few miles of paved roads in the park and, although they traverse pleasant forests amid hilly, rugged terrain, there are no spectacular points of interest along these roads. Similarly, the park is not geared toward the casual outdoor stroll.

Across the Green River, which cuts through much of the park, the road soon ends and there are miles and miles of trails through the picturesque bluffs of Kentucky's countryside. These trails are long and unimproved, so they will be of interest primarily to overnight hikers and wildlife enthusiasts. The cave is definitely the thing to see here, so we'll get on to that right now.

Mammoth Cave National Park

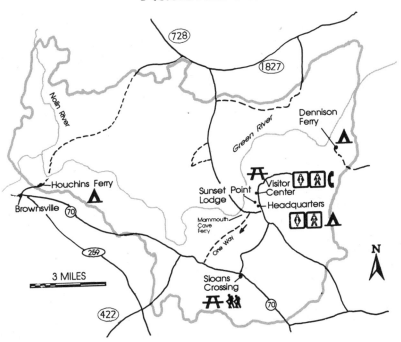

Special Activities

The major activity in the park is taking one or more of the several **ranger-conducted tours** of the cave. These last from just over an hour to about five hours. No self-guided options are available. It is wise to consider taking more than one tour since they generally visit different areas of the cave. We suggest you make reservations before arriving at the park for all cave tours as they become sold out quickly.

The 1¼-hour **"Frozen Niagara" Tour** covers about one mile and requires almost no effort. It passes many of the cave's most famous and beautiful formations, including the one that gives this particular tour its name. This is a good introduction to the cave, but don't let it be your only venture underground, for the Frozen Niagara does not give you a real sense of how vast the subterranean rooms can be. The **Travertine Tour** is an even shorter version of the Frozen Niagara, especially for the elderly. There are also special tours for the disabled. Inquire at the visitor center.

The **Historical Tour** takes about two hours and covers two miles. It, too, is not very strenuous, although there are a few parts that might be difficult for larger visitors. To really"experience Mammoth Cave, you should take the **Scenic Tour** (sometimes called the Half-Day Tour), which lasts five hours and takes you through four miles of passages. There are several long climbs and descents but, unless you are disabled or really out of shape, the pace is not difficult. This tour makes a stop for lunch in a section of the cave known as the Snowball Dining Room. Since this tour includes a large part of the Frozen Niagara Tour, you really need only take the Scenic and Historic tours to see the cave adequately. These two do not cover any of the same territory.

Real caving enthusiasts can take one of several more difficult lantern tours through primitive portions of the cave system.

The park's visitor center has interesting exhibits and will also provide you with information on tour departure points. Reservations can be made here as well.

An often overlooked but worthwhile attraction in the park is the 75-minute **cruise along the Green River**, which gives visitors a good idea of the terrain surrounding the cave. Trips leave from the boat dock adjacent to the cable ferry ($). Purchase tickets at the visitor center, which is only a few miles from the dock.

Accommodations

Attractive lodging is available right on the park grounds near the visitor center at **Mammoth Cave Hotel**. This facility has 106 motor-inn type rooms (M). Their phone number is (502) 758-2328. For those who prefer to stay outside the park, there are many motels (including nationwide chain affiliates) in the nearby towns of Park City, Cave City and Glasgow.

Dining

The restaurant in the **Mammoth Cave Hotel** is quite nice. Again, the nearby towns will provide numerous alternatives from fast-food to full-service restaurants. If you are going on the Scenic Tour, you should take advantage of the lunch stop in the **Snowball Room**. It is little more than a cafeteria, but the experience of eating in the cave will make up for the lack of culinary niceties.

Where Do We Go From Here?

As an extension to *Suggested Trip 1*, Mammoth Cave is relatively far from other parks in this book. But it is close to the historic and scenic attractions of the Kentucky Bluegrass country, to central Tennessee or to the rugged Appalachian region of eastern Kentucky.

24

Mesa Verde
National Park

Mesa Verde was established primarily because it is one of the nation's most important archaeological preserves, but it also happens to be an area of outstanding natural beauty. Mesa Verde means "Green Table," and that is exactly what it looks like from a distance: a huge flat-topped plateau covered with forest. The plateau is roughly 2,000 feet above the level of the surrounding valley. On the top of the mesa are many small, deep canyons, featuring large and well-preserved remains of cliff dwellings. The area was inhabited as early as 500 A.D., but the remains that are visible today date from around the 13th century. It is fascinating to see how the "primitive" cultures that lived here adapted their homes to the difficult environment and terrain. A visit to Mesa Verde is one that will leave a deep impression on you, for its beauty as well as its history.

Facts & Figures

LOCATION/GATEWAYS/GETTING THERE: Mesa Verde is 10 miles east of Cortez or 36 miles west of Durango on US 160 in extreme southwestern Colorado. From Denver it is about 380 miles via I-25 and US 160.

YEAR ESTABLISHED: One of the nation's oldest national parks, Mesa Verde's value was realized early on, and it received its status in 1906.

ADMISSION FEE: $5.

CLIMATE/WHEN TO GO: The park is open all year, but the facilities operate on a very limited basis in winter when it is cold and there is sometimes a heavy snow cover. Many of the ruins have guided tours during the spring and fall when the park is less crowded, but are on a self-guiding basis during the busy summer season. Summer temperatures are comfortable because of the high elevation (over 8,000 feet), so it is a good idea to visit during this period, as it may often be chilly in spring and fall.

ADDRESS/TELEPHONE: Superintendent, Mesa Verde National Park, PO Box 8, Mesa Verde CO 81330. (303) 529-4465.

Auto Tour/Short Stops

Virtually all of the ruins and the best of the park's scenery can easily be seen on a driving tour.

From the entrance off US 160, the park road travels about 20 miles before reaching the top of the mesa. During this journey the road rises sharply and the curves become increasingly frequent and pronounced. After passing through a long tunnel there begins a series of dramatic switchbacks that provide panoramic vistas of the route you have travelled and what lies ahead. But keep your eyes on the road – the best views are at the **Montezuma Valley Overlook** and, shortly after that, via a short spur road leading to **Park Point**, perhaps the best view in the park. **The North Rim Overlook** follows within a short distance. Here, you will be at an elevation of 8,572 feet and have a fantastic view extending into four different states.

Soon afterwards you reach the top of the mesa in an area known as Far View. The park's large, modern visitor center is here and contains, along with visitor facilities, an excellent exhibit on the culture of the cliff dwellers. This will be especially interesting to first-time visitors. Back on the road, after passing the nearby **Far View Ruins**, the road reaches the **Chapin Mesa**. A fine museum here details the development of the Anasazi Indian culture. A short walk from the museum takes you to the **Spruce Tree Ruin**. Although it takes only a few minutes, the climb back up is quite steep. But it is well worth the effort because Spruce Tree Ruin is one of the best-preserved cliff dwellings in the park – and one of the more accessible. If you decide not to visit it, you can at least get an excellent view of the ruin from the mesa's rim.

Immediately south from Spruce Tree, the road divides into two loops, each about six miles long. These loops lead to excellent vantage points of the dwellings from a series of canyon rim lookouts. If you bring along a pair of binoculars you can see details of the dwelling interiors without actually going into them. (Some are not open to visitors so it is a good idea to have those binoculars handy in any case.) In the order that you will approach them, your stops should include the **Square Tower House** (viewed from the canyon rim only); a short walk through a series of pithouses and pueblos on the mesa's surface; and a fabulous view of the **Cliff Palace**, the park's largest and most famous dwelling, best seen from the **Sun Point** and, finally, the **Sun Temple**.

The second loop passes along Cliff Palace and Balcony House (see the next section for details on these) as well as the Fewkes Canyon ruins.

Including the access road drive, the two loops, view stops and short walk to Spruce Tree House, the Auto Tour portion of your visit to Mesa Verde will require between three and four well-spent hours.

Getting Out/Longer Stops

While the Auto Tour is a relaxing and excellent introduction to Mesa Verde, it only included entry into one of the major dwellings. For the more adventurous, the Cliff Palace and Balcony House can be explored on self-guided tours. Cliff Palace is the easier of the two, but it is still much more difficult than Spruce Tree House because it requires ascending and descending several long ladders to reach the interior. In allocating time for your visit, figure about one hour for each structure that you will be exploring in greater detail.

Special Activities

A side trip available only during the summer between 8 AM and 4:30 PM is the ride to adjacent **Wetherill Mesa**. The trip encompasses beautiful scenery and cliff dwellings not visible from Chapin Mesa's main loop roads. The 12-mile road is steep, with many curves. No trailers are allowed. Although the sights are similar to those at Chapin Mesa, Wetherill is far less crowded. If you have the time (three hours at a minimum) and feel like seeing ruins in an isolated setting, then the trip will prove worthwhile.

Accommodations

Because it takes the better part of a day to see Mesa Verde properly, you may well want to remain overnight in the park. If so, then the **Far View Lodge** is an ideal place to stay. This modern and attractive 150-room motor inn has much nicer facilities than are available in many national parks and there are also spectacular views from the rooms' private sun porches (M). Call (303) 529-4465 for reservations. Lodging is also available in nearby Mancos, with more choices in Cortez. Durango, although a bit farther, has the widest variety of accommodations in the region.

Dining

The **Far View Lodge** contains an excellent full-service restaurant and there is also a good cafeteria in the visitor center. The cafeteria has a wider selection and better food than is usually found in national parks. Cortez and Durango also have a vast array of eating places ranging from fast food to elegant gourmet dining.

Where Do We Go From Here?

As you will probably be using fairly distant Denver as your gateway for visiting Mesa Verde, you should really try to do all of *Suggested Trip 3*. At a minimum, a visit to southern Colorado, in addition to Mesa Verde, should include **Durango** and the **Silverton** and/or the **Million Dollar Highway, Black Canyon of the Gunnison** and the **Curecanti National Recreation Area**, as well as **Colorado Springs** and **Canon City**.

25

Mount Rainier National Park

Perhaps the most famous peak of the Pacific Northwest's Cascade Range, Mount Rainier is a dormant, but not extinct, ice-clad volcanic mountain. At 14,410 feet, it is a giant, though certainly not the highest of mountains. But it is Mount Rainier's sheer bulk and the fact that it is set apart from its neighboring peaks in the range that make it the dominant landmark of the region. So much does it dominate the surrounding landscape, that it is commonly referred to by locals simply as "The Mountain." Seeming to float in the air, it is visible from over 100 miles away on clear days. It towers more than 8,000 feet above the surrounding terrain. Its legendary beauty is as great as its overpowering size.

Rainier's 27 glaciers cover more than 34 square miles, making it the largest single-peak glacial system in the lower 48 states. The smooth glacial ice hides what is really an extremely rugged mountain composed of many jagged surfaces. Other scenery in the park is equally impressive – heavily forested up to an altitude of about 5,000 feet, the landscape then becomes covered with absolutely magnificent meadows of wildflowers, a feature second only to the mountain itself in attracting visitors. Then, above the timberline, at about 6,500 feet, there is only rock and ice. Its beauty and awe-inspiring presence cannot really be described or imagined. It is our good fortune that Mount Rainier National Park is highly accessible, so let us begin our journey.

Facts & Figures

LOCATION/GATEWAYS/GETTING THERE: Mount Rainier is in west-central Washington, less than two hours from the city of Seattle.

There are approaches from all four directions but the two primary routes (coming from the Seattle-Tacoma metropolitan area) are SR 410 from I-5 via the town of Enumclaw (White River entrance), or SRs 7 and 706 from Tacoma (Nisqually entrance). Coming from the south, US 12 leads into SR 123 (the Ohanapecosh entrance); and SR 410 also approaches the park from the east (the direction of Yakima) at the Chinook Pass entrance.

YEAR ESTABLISHED: Known to the Indians since prehistoric times, the great mountain was first sighted by European explorers in the year 1792. Extensive exploration of Mount Rainier did not begin until the 1850s and it became America's fourth national park in 1899.

SIZE: 235,404 acres (or 368 square miles).

ADMISSION FEE: $5.

CLIMATE/WHEN TO GO: Although open all year, many roads are closed by heavy winter snows until the middle of June. Only the Nisqually entrance is open throughout the year. The comfortably cool summer season lasts from the time that all roads open until August or perhaps early September. This is the only practical time for most visitors, especially first-timers, even though the park is at its most crowded. Very simply, at all other times of the year there will be portions of the park that you cannot get to see and these areas should not be missed. While crowded roads may be a negative, the other advantage of a summer visit is that this is the time when views are least likely to be obscured by clouds. Despite the Pacific Northwest's reputation for rain and overcast skies, it has surprisingly dry summers.

ADDRESS/TELEPHONE: Superintendent, Mount Rainier National Park, Tahoma Woods-Star Route, Ashford, WA 98304. (206) 569-2211.

Mount Rainier National Park

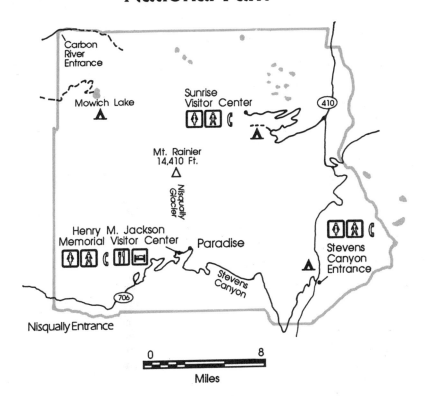

Auto Tour/Short Stops

Although the park road system does not climb up Mount Rainier itself, or even surround it on all sides, it is surprisingly easy to see the park's many highlights from in or near your car. The main road network, starting from the Nisqually entrance, runs through the southern part of the park (Nisqually-Paradise and Stevens Canyon Roads); and then along the eastern edge of the park (East Side Road and Mather Memorial Parkway). These, along with one major spur road (Sunrise/White River Road) will be the key to your trip. Other roads in the park are unpaved and difficult to negotiate. It is most logical to begin your tour at either the Nisqually or White River entrances but, for those coming from either the south or east, you can actually begin at any entrance and see everything with a little extra mileage for back-tracking. Frequent overlooks make it possible to see the best scenery no matter which direction you are traveling. We'll follow a south and then westerly route in this description (i.e., beginning from the northeast corner of the park), because this is the way many people will arrive if they start their trip in Seattle.

About four miles after coming through the north entrance there will be a cutoff for the White River Road, which later becomes the Sunrise Road. (Get used to such shifts; it is common for the road to receive a new name as it enters a different region of the park.) This spur, with an approximate one-way distance of 15 miles, leads to the magnificent **Sunrise area** of the park. It is a detour that is too often missed by visitors simply because it is not on the main road, but the half-hour it takes to drive each way is certainly well worth the time, as you will soon see. About two-thirds of the way to Sunrise, there is a parking area called **Sunrise Point**. Perched in the middle of a long, gentle switchback, it is the first of many unforgettable stops you will make. This is where you will likely first fully appreciate the immensity of Mount Rainier. Amazing views of the snow- and ice-covered mountain, including the peak, await you here. Do not fret if there is some cloudiness, especially in the morning, for in summer it will likely clear before the day is out. In fact, if it is still cloud-covered on your way up to Sunrise there is a good chance it will have cleared by the time you pass this spot on your way back to the main road. The small **Sunrise Visitor Center** here (one of four centers in the park) that has exhibits explaining the topography of the area and you can take a brief walk in the surrounding wildflower meadow, aglow with color in the shadow of the great mountain and its icy blanket.

Sunrise is the closest you can get to the summit by car. At 6,400 feet, Sunrise Visitor Center is more than a thousand feet higher than the more heavily visited Paradise headquarters area. Now reverse your route to the East Side Road, then continue south. Once you are past the Chinook Pass entrance road, the road changes names again, now becoming the Stevens Canyon Road. It enters a more scenic section of the park than was visible from the East Side Road (which is generally in a thick forest that blocks most views of Rainier and more distant mountains). Stop for the views at **Backbone Ridge** and at **Box Canyon**, where there is a dizzying view into the waterfall-filled canyon. **Reflection Lake** is another overlook that shouldn't be missed. These stops are all within a short distance of one another and provide some of the most breathtaking views of Mount Rainier itself while also showcasing the park's other beautiful features – canyons, rivers, lakes and waterfalls. Distant peaks of the Cascade Range are also visible. The road appears as a thin ribbon dwarfed by the surrounding landscape, as the switchbacks place the highway both above and beneath you. It is a dramatic sight.

You will then come upon the junction to Paradise. Take the spur road which climbs sharply for a short time to Paradise Village, site of the park headquarters and the majority of visitor services. Because of the traffic in this area and the steep grades, use low gear. At Paradise be sure to visit the modernistic visitor center, perched at the foot of the Nisqually Glacier. The circular building provides a magnificent 360° panorama. Opportunities for pleasant strolls through the Paradise area's many wildflower meadows are plentiful and you will be rewarded with clear views of some of the park's major glaciers. (See the next section for detail.)

Leaving Paradise, pick up the Nisqually-Paradise Road going westbound. The first stop on this leg of the route is **Narada Falls**. A brief walk from the parking area descends to the bottom of a ravine and the foot of the very picturesque falls. Just beyond here the road brings you to **Ricksecker Point**, one of the most beautiful of all the viewpoints along the road system. Next you will approach **Longmire**, where there is an historical museum with interesting exhibits about the native population. Shortly before reaching the southwestern (or Nisqually) exit of the park is the site of the **Kautz Mudflow**. This mud slide in the 1920's did extensive damage here. You would be hard-pressed to see true evidence of the damage today for nature has done an outstanding job of rejuvenation. Within a short walk are exhibits about the mudflow and nice views of streams and wildflowers, all in the foreground of Mount Rainier itself.

This concludes the auto portion of your tour. The drive, with breaks to stop, look and walk, should take you about six hours.

Getting Out/Longer Stops

Although there are more than 300 miles of trails in the park, many of these are difficult, long trails that lead upward toward or around the summit and over its glaciers. As such, they are not for the casual visitor. But many other trails are easier. In the Sunrise area, the half-mile **Emmons Vista Trail** provides excellent views of Mount Rainier and the Emmons Glacier. It takes about a half-hour. The 1½-mile **Sourdough Ridge Nature Trail** is another walk that does not require any unusual amount of effort. Many varieties of flowers and plants will be encountered and are labeled for easy identification. Other trails at Sunrise range from three to six miles and may take up to four hours. These are more extensive versions of the Emmons Vista Trail. Paradise provides the greatest number of opportunities for exploration on foot. The **Nisqually Vista Trail**, 1½ miles round-trip, is the easiest in the area and one of the best. Besides providing an excellent view of the Nisqually Glacier, this trail is well-known for the beautiful wildflower meadows that it passes through. Allow one hour. The **Skyline Trail** is a more strenuous, 4½-mile loop requiring about four hours. Boots are advisable as you are likely to encounter snow and ice. Several other trails are spurs off the Skyline Trail or variations of it.

There are also several trails of varying length and difficulty departing from the Longmire Visitor Center, but none of these is as popular or as rewarding as those in either Sunrise or Paradise.

Finally, if you have a lot of time to spare (minimum of six hours) you might consider the six-mile round-trip to an area of unusual beauty – an underground palace of ice, the brilliant blue **Ice Caves**. Inquire at the Paradise Visitor Center before embarking because access to the cave is sometimes blocke by heavy snow and ice.

Accommodations

The Paradise Inn, an older but comfortable 125-room lodge, is the largest hotel within the park itself. This massive timber building is quite famous (B to M), and worth a look even if you aren't staying there. The 25-room **National Park Inn** in Longmire is another historic structure (M). Nearby towns with lodging are at Ashwood (west of the park), Enumclaw (north), and Packwood (south). Facilities at the latter are modest, but these towns provide convenient access to a major park entrance. In-park reservations are by Mount Rainier Guest Services, (206) 569-2400.

Dining

The Paradise Inn has an excellent restaurant. There is also a quick, inexpensive cafeteria at the visitor center in Paradise, which is a good place for lunch. Restaurants are plentiful in all the nearby towns that have lodging.

Where Do We Go From Here?

Trip 8 in the final part of this book is an excellent way to see the scenic parts of Washington. However, if you are pressed for time, Mount Rainier can be done as part of an overnight trip from Seattle. Depending upon how much time is available to you, additions can then be made to the **Olympic Peninsula**, the **North Cascades** or, possibly, **Mount St. Helens** (which is included in *Trip 9*). If you want to combine some city sightseeing, then Mount Rainier can be an accompaniment not only to Seattle but to the nearby and beautiful Canadian cities of Vancouver and Victoria, British Columbia.

Finally, there is a large section of Mount Rainier National Park (the western edge of the park) that is seldom seen except by the backcountry enthusiast. Although I do not suggest it for most casual visitors, there are several unpaved roads that provide access to this forested section of the park.

26

Mount Rushmore National Memorial

Mount Rushmore National Memorial is part of the highly scenic Black Hills region. In fact, the memorial fits in so well with its natural surroundings that it almost seems as if the carving was there by an act of nature more than by the hand of man. Mount Rushmore is a symbol of America every bit as much as the Statue of Liberty. It's a bit out of the way compared to that, but worth every effort. It is an experience you will never forget. The idea of the memorial was born in 1923, but actual construction did not begin until four years after that and its completion took another 14 years. The sculptor, Gutzon Borglum, selected the site because the 6,000-foot mountain dominated the surrounding terrain and because it faced the sun for most of the day. The heads of George Washington, Thomas Jefferson, Abraham Lincoln, and Theodore Roosevelt are each 60 feet high and carved in such intricate detail that the emotions of the subjects are clearly evident to the observer. The colossal carvings are 1,400 feet above the visitor center and the adjacent viewing areas.

Facts & Figures

LOCATION/GATEWAYS/GETTING THERE: In the middle of the Black Hills of southwestern South Dakota, Mount Rushmore is near Rapid City on SR 244 and is accessible from that city by US 16 and 16A. There aren't any large cities within 350 miles of the memorial, but there is regularly scheduled air service into Rapid City.

YEAR ESTABLISHED: Dedicated as a national memorial in August, 1927.

SIZE: 1,278 acres (or 2 square miles). Tiny, but there is much to see.

ADMISSION FEE: None.

CLIMATE/WHEN TO GO: The memorial is open all year, but extended visiting hours and some activities are available only from Memorial Day through Labor Day. The beginning and end of this main season is marked by cool days and chilly nights. During the summer it is quite warm but still has comfortably cool evenings. Sun is the rule in summer, except for heavy and frequent afternoon thunderstorms. Bring a jacket for activities in the evening.

ADDRESS/TELEPHONE: Superintendent, Mount Rushmore National Memorial, P.O. Box 268, Keystone, SD 57751. (605) 574-2523.

Auto Tour/Getting Out

We'll combine these two categories, as there are no extended walks available and, beyond the parking area at the Memorial entrance, there are no roads open to the public. Nor are they needed – just park your car and walk! Do note, however, that some of the access roads are narrow and have tunnels. Trailers are not allowed in the memorial; if you have one, leave it in the town of Keystone. Actually, you will be far better off without a trailer when traveling throughout the Black Hills.

Before describing the memorial, I should mention one short side trip that provides a fantastic distant view of the carving. This is available from the **Norbeck Overlook** on Iron Mountain Road (US 16), about five miles south of the memorial. Don't miss it! Not only is the view great, but the road, an engineering marvel, is an exciting drive.

Climbing on Mount Rushmore is strictly prohibited.

Special Activities

The activities here all have to do with viewing the sculpture. The Presidents are best seen from special terraces and marked observation points near the visitor center. A paved path, flanked by the flags of the states, leads through the entire area. The visitor center has numerous exhibits and films on the memorial, the lives of the Presidents on the carving, and the fascinating process of how it was created. From Memorial Day to Labor Day a talk is given by rangers at 9:00 PM. every evening in the amphitheater directly beneath the carving. Then, from 9:30 until 10:30 (from 8:00 to 8:30 during the remainder of the year), the heads are illuminated. You will be seated on rather cold benches, so you might want to bring along a cushion or blanket to keep your bottom warm.

Finally, the **sculptor's studio** on the grounds displays tools actually used in the carving process. It is only open during the summer season.

Accommodations

There is no overnight lodging in the memorial (and no camping). However, a large assortment of lodgings in all price ranges is available in surrounding Black Hills communities such as Keystone, Custer, Hill City, and Rapid City.

Dining

A fine cafeteria, the **Buffalo Dining Room,** is in the same building as the visitor center. Besides having very good food at reasonable prices, the large picture windows look out on the carving itself. So if you can arrange it, plan on dining with the four presidents. The towns mentioned above under Accommodations also offer a wide choice of restaurants.

Where Do We Go From Here?

Suggested Trip 2 is the logical way to see the memorial. Since your entire visit will take no more than a couple of hours (plus the evening program), at a minimum you should see the rest of the **Black Hills** and the **Badlands National Park** in the same trip.

27

Mount St. Helens National Volcanic Monument

Many of us still vividly remember that fateful morning in May of 1980 when, after several months of rumbling and threatening, Mount St. Helens blew its top – sending over a thousand feet of its peak and much of the north face of the mountain high into the air in an explosion of unimaginable force. Ash and darkened skies blanketed hundreds of square miles downwind as far as Spokane. Everything in the immediate path of the blast was instantaneously destroyed by the combination of intense heat and winds of several hundred miles per hour. It was nature at its most furious. What had before been one of the jewels of the Cascade Range was turned into a barren wasteland. Visiting Mount St. Helens today, the destruction is still clearly evident, though signs of life are rapidly reappearing in the fertile land. It is a strange world, with a unique kind of beauty.

Facts & Figures

LOCATION/GATEWAYS/GETTING THERE: The monument is northeast of Portland, Oregon, via I-5 and SR 504 (west side) or via I-5 and SR 503 and then forest service roads (details later) on the east side. Allow about two hours from Portland to the volcanic area. It can also be reached from Seattle via I-5 south to SR 504 or, on the east side, I-5 to US 12 onto forest roads at the town of Randle.

YEAR ESTABLISHED: The area became the nation's only national volcanic monument in 1982.

SIZE: 110,000 acres (or 172 square miles).

ADMISSION FEES: There is no charge.

CLIMATE/WHEN TO GO: The west side is open all year, but the east side roads are only open from the middle of June to late October, depending upon the weather. If you intend to see the east side, then you must go in summer. Actually, this is the best time for either side because it is drier and more comfortable than other times of the year.

ADDRESS/TELEPHONE: The monument is administered by the United States Forest Service, rather than the National Park Service. The forest serice has several information centers throughout the monument area. The best bet is to write the headquarters. Address inquiries to Mount St. Helens National Volcanic Monument, 42218 N.E. Yale Bridge Road, Amboy WA 98601. (360) 750-3900 or (360) 750-3903 for 24-hour recorded information.

Auto Tour/Short Stops

The monument is physically divided into two main areas, the west and east sides. They are not directly connected. It requires driving a long distance to get from one side to the other so we'll consider them separately. (Due to time limitations, most people will do only one or the other.) 1996 marked the completion of many years of construction projects to improve visitor facilities and roads that provide access to previously inaccessible areas, including some of the most staggering sights.

West Side

This is the most accessible portion and is, thanks to the aforementioned improvements, a very rewarding experience for the visitor. Use the Castle Rock exit (#49) from I-5. SR 504 is the road leading into the monument. Milepost markers (MP) indicated in parentheses show distances from the town of Castle Rock. The route is officially known as the Spirit Lake Memorial Highway.

Mount St. Helens
National Volcanic Monument

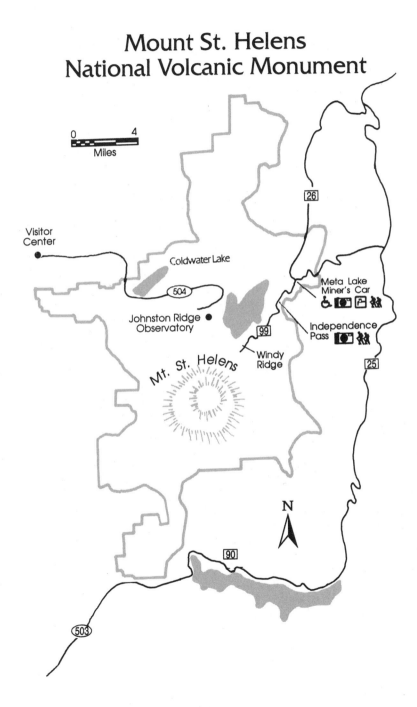

The **Mount St. Helens Visitor Center** (MP 5) describes the volcanos of the Cascade Range as well as the events leading up to and following the eruption of Mt. St. Helens. Further along at Maple Flats (MP 19) there is a small A-frame cabin buried in a mudflow from the eruption. The **Sediment Retention Structure Viewpoint** (MP 22) is a dam that holds back muddy and ash-laden materials from entering nearby rivers and streams. A short walk leads to the dam. At the **Hoffstadt Bluffs** (MP 27) there is a small visitor center and excellent views of both the "new" Mount St. Helens towering above you, and the mud of the "old" mountain top that ended up here in a mudslide, 15 miles from the point of eruption. After crossing the Hoffstadt Creek Bridge you enter the eruption's blast zone and will catch glimpses of standing dead trees among the living ones that have been recently planted. A more impressive reminder of the damage done to the forest can be seen from the **Elk Rock Viewpoint** (MP 37).

At the **Coldwater Ridge Visitor Center** (MP 43) you'll see excellent views of the crater and lava dome as well as of the beautiful **Toutle River Valley** and it's two volcano-formed lakes. Exhibits here describe events and the natural recovery process following an eruption. Two miles further on you get a close-up view of **Coldwater Lake**. Finally, the **Johnston Ridge Observatory** (MP 52) promises an unparalled close-up view into the crater itself. There are also exhibits. Return the opposite way on SR 504. Your visit to the west side should take a minimum of five hours.

East Side

From Portland, exit I-5 at SR 503 in Woodland and follow this scenic route along rivers and lakes until you reach forest route (FR) 90. Turn off FR 90 at FR 25 northbound and remain on that road until its junction with FR 99. This will take you to **Spirit Lake** and provides the most breathtaking vistas of the area. It will lead you to those sections where the destruction was greatest and is still most evident. There are several observation points along this road, including **Bear Meadow, Meta Lake,** and **Independence Pass**, before you finally reach the end of the line at **Windy Ridge**. While at Windy Ridge you will have a panorama of the volcano's destructive force. This is the closest you can get to the crater by car. The roads are narrow and twisting, but it is well worth the effort at the end as you stand there, look, and imagine. Also on this road at Meta Lake is the **Miner's Car**. This car was in the blast area when the volcano erupted, and it has been fenced off and left as a sample of what nature can do. The heat literally stripped off the paint.

Work your way back on SR 99 to the junction of FR 26. This forest road will take you past Ryan Lake, an area that was also heavily devastated. The tops of trees have been cut off and are all leaning away from the blast. FR 26 will take you back to FR 25. From here you can head south to retrace your route or go north on US 12 at Randle. This route can either take you westbound to I-5 or to Mount Rainier National Park if you travel east. Just reverse the itinerary if you come from this direction (i.e., from Seattle or Mt. Rainier) to start your visit to Mount St. Helens. The east side driving tour will take about five hours.

If you intend to do both sides, the best way to connect them is by taking US 12 back to I-5 and then head south to Silver Lake (i.e., start with the east side and work your way around to the west). This additional 100-plus miles will take more than two hours.

Getting Out/Longer Stops

Most of the trails on the east side involve extensive climbing, but there are a few along FR 99, notably at Independence Pass. These can be done in an hour or so and will give you additional vistas of the area without unusual effort. No trails into the crater itself are open to the public, due to the danger of volcanic activity.

Special Activities

There are some **guided walks and hikes** that you can inquire about. An especially interesting one is the half-hour tour of **Ape Cave**, a huge lava tube, departing from the junction of FR 83 and FR 90 on the monument's southern edge.

Accommodations & Dining

Before the eruption this was a primitive wilderness area and, for the most part, it remains so today. There are no lodging facilities in the monument, but the towns of Cougar and Packwood are within easy reach for the east side visitor. If you are visiting the west side, then a number of towns along I-5 will give you a good choice of places to stay. These include Woodland, Kalama, Kelso, and

Longview (all between Portland and SR 504) or Chehalis and
Centralia north of SR 504. Another alternative is to leave Portland
in the morning, spend the entire day circling the monument and
then return to Portland in the evening. The accommodation restrictions apply to dining as well, although there are snacks available at
several points within the volcanic area on both sides and adjacent
to the monument borders.

Where Do We Go From Here?

Suggested Trip 9 includes Mount St. Helens. The trip has Portland as
its gateway and that is the most logical starting point for venturing
out to the monument. However, you could extend *Trip 8* to include
it as well, since it is not far from the southern entrance to Mount
Rainier National Park. Of course, a combination of the two is
possible, leaving off some of the attractions at the northern and
southern ends to keep the trip's length manageable.

28

North Cascades & Ross Lake

These two adjacent areas (Ross Lake Recreation Area is an L-shaped strip of land that separates the northern and southern portions of North Cascades), contain absolutely majestic ice-covered mountain peaks and canyons. There are more than 300 glaciers in North Cascades alone. In addition, rushing rivers and brilliant green glacial lakes add to the breathtaking vistas that seem to be everywhere you look. Many of the park's peaks are over 8,000 feet and the highest is 9,127-foot Mount Shuksan. These tower above the valley where the North Cascades Highway (SR 20) runs, taking you into this pristine wilderness of unimaginable beauty. Many of the lakes in the Ross Lake National Recreation Area are the result of hydroelectric projects that supply power for Seattle.

Facts & Figures

LOCATION/GATEWAYS/GETTING THERE: It is about 120 miles from the city of Seattle to the heart of the Ross Lake area, an easy drive via I-5 to Burlington and then via the highly scenic North Cascades Highway (SR 20). The trip from Seattle takes less than three hours.

YEAR ESTABLISHED: North Cascades was created in 1968, as was Ross Lake.

SIZE: North Cascades is 504,781 acres (or 789 square miles). Ross Lake is 117,574 acres (or 184 square miles).

ADMISSION FEE: There is no charge for entering either area.

CLIMATE/WHEN TO GO: Summer is the best time to go as this is when the sun is most likely to be out and the temperatures are most comfortable. The road is open from April through the middle of November, depending upon the amount of snowfall.

ADDRESS/TELEPHONE: Information for both areas can be obtained from the Superintendent, North Cascades National Park, 2105 State Highway 20, Sedro Wooley, WA 98284. (206) 856-5700.

Auto Tour/Short Stops

The scenic features of North Cascades and Ross Lake are similar, which is understandable if you look at a map – Ross Lake National Recreation Area lies right in the middle of the park. Essentially, they can be considered as one. There are no paved roads in the North Cascades, whereas SR 20 provides easy access to what nature has to offer in the vast area of Ross Lake. We'll describe some ways to see the interior of the North Cascades a bit later.

About 20 miles before you get to the recreation area, the scenery on SR 20 becomes quite splendid. There are mountain vistas, rivers and canyons, some of which can be easily seen from roadside rest areas. As the highway cuts through the recreation area itself, the views become even more spectacular. When you reach the **Diablo** area there are several short nature trails and attractive gardens that have been developed in connection with the Skagit Hydroelectric project (see Special Activities). Ross Lake itself is visible from points just past Diablo. I suggest that you continue 25 miles past the recreation area (still on SR 20) until you reach the **Washington Pass**. Although the pass is actually in the neighboring Okanogan National Forest, there is a scenic overlook here that faces the peaks of the southern North Cascades and it is one of the most dramatic views available. A short trail leads to the overlook at an elevation of 5,500 feet. The scenery along the entire stretch of road in this area justifies the additional mileage. On the way back you will get an excellent view of Liberty Bell Mountain as you reenter the park. This is an area of especially rugged peaks.

Allow about 2½ hours for the driving portion of your visit.

North Cascades National Park/ Ross Lake National Recreation Area

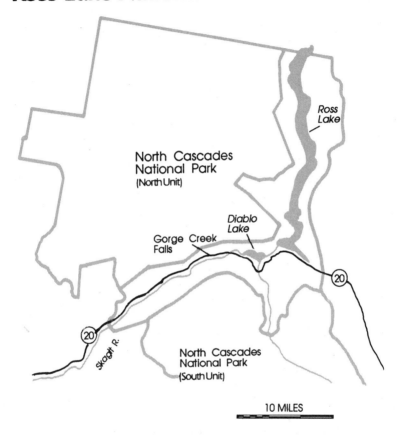

Ross Lake

North Cascades National Park (North Unit)

Diablo Lake

Gorge Creek Falls

20

20

Skagit R.

North Cascades National Park (South Unit)

10 MILES

Special Activities

North Cascades is not a highly developed park, and even better-developed Ross Lake has relatively few ranger-conducted activities. But the Seattle City Light Company, which operates the hydro project, conducts a fantastic four-hour trip that includes lunch or dinner. The tour operates three times daily and should not be missed. After a brief orientation film you take a ride to the top of **Sourdough Mountain** on an unusual piece of equipment – a large open platform. During your 560-foot ascent you will have great views of mountain peaks, glacial valleys and emerald-colored lakes. At the top a short walk leads to a boat dock and you will take a 20-minute cruise to one of the power houses in the huge hydroelectric project – all amid wonderful scenery. Then you return the same way you came. Very little time is spent in the "industrial" portion of the project. Short of back-packing into the interior of North Cascades, this is the best way to see the natural beauty of this area. Reservations are required. Call (206) 625-3030 for tour information ($).

There is one other activity that might interest you, but it requires almost 200 miles of additional driving, round-trip. Continue on SR 20 past the Washington Pass Overlook described earlier, then onto SR 153 and US 97 until you arrive at the town of Chelan. From here, there are all-day **steamer trips** on Lake Chelan that will actually take you into the southernmost portion of North Cascades National Park ($). The scenery is absolutely beautiful, but whether you want to include it in your itinerary will depend on how much time you have. The trip takes an extra 1½ days.

Accommodations

Diablo Lake Resort has 18 attractive cottages. It is in the town of Diabl, part of Ross Lake Recreation Area, and it is the only lodging along the road corridor in the two scenic areas (M). More varied accommodations are available in Sedro Wooley and in Burlington, off I-5. Chelan also has good facilities.

Dining

Food service is available at **Diablo Lake Resort** and in the towns mentioned above. Roadside restaurants are also scattered along SR 20 in towns not far from the recreation area. A delicious family-style dinner is served in a dining room upon completion of your Skagit-City Light Tour (but you must be on the tour to use the dining room).

Where Do We Go From Here?

Trip 8 described in the last section of this book includes both Ross Lake and the North Cascades. However, its relative proximity to Seattle means that it can be included in a number of alternative trips using Seattle as a base. Certainly **Mount Rainier** and **Olympic National Parks** and the **San Juan Islands** can be included. Also, once you get back to the junction of I-5 it is extremely close to the Canadian border. So, trips to **Vancouver** and, perhaps, **Victoria** are also an opotion.

29

Olympic National Park

Occupying the major portion of the Olympic Peninsula, this is one of the wildest areas in the nation. In fact, the road network is deliberately confined to just a few miles near the edge of the park in several places, so that the wilderness will be preserved for all time. The landscape here is some of the most diverse in the national park system – from 57 miles of rocky beaches to glacier-covered mountain peaks. And, of course, there is the rain forest for which the area is so famous. The centerpiece of the park is 7,965-foot Mount Olympus, a great glacial mountain which seems even taller because it rises so abruptly from the nearby shoreline. The park boasts extraordinary meadows of wildflowers and dozens of varieties of trees, including some of America's tallest. This great diversity has made Olympic not only a national park, treasured by America, but a World Heritage Park because of its great biological and geological significance. There is something for everyone in Olympic National Park, one of America's largest parks and among its most ravishing beauties!

Facts & Figures

LOCATION/GATEWAYS/GETTING THERE: Encircled by US 101 on northwest Washington's Olympic Peninsula, the headquarters area of the park is at Port Angeles, on the north coast. To this point it is 178 miles from Seattle via I-5 and US 101, a drive of just under four hours. It is less than a hundred miles if you take the ferry from Seattle to Bremerton and then take SRs 3 and 104 into US 101. The driving time will be cut in half on this route, but the total travel time is not significantly different because of the ferry trip. However, this is certainly a more relaxing and scenic way to get to the park. Ferry service is frequent.

YEAR ESTABLISHED: First sighted by European explorers in 1774, the interior was not really traversed until the 1890s. The area became a national monument in 1909 and, finally, a national park in 1938.

SIZE: 914,576 miles (or 1,429 square miles), three-fourths the size of Delaware.

ADMISSION FEE: $5.

CLIMATE/WHEN TO GO: The Olympic Peninsula has mild winters and cool summers. It is one of the wettest areas in the United States, with much of the rain forest sections receiving over 150 inches of precipitation a year and more than 200 inches usually falling on Mount Olympus itself. However, most of this comes in the form of winter snowfalls and rains in spring and fall. The summer is relatively dry. Combine this with the fact that many roads are closed from October through late June, and it is clear that the best time for a visit is during July, August or early September.

ADDRESS/TELEPHONE: Superintendent, Olympic National Park, 600 East Park Avenue, Port Angeles, WA 98362. (206) 452-0330.

Auto Tour/Short Stops

The network of paved roads does not penetrate the interior of the park, and even the unpaved roads, which are often difficult to negotiate, still only skirt the edges of this vast domain. (Trailers, by the way, are not recommended for visitors to the park.) Yet, US 101, which surrounds most of the perimeter of the park, has several roads leading off of it that provide good access to many of the most significant of Olympic's features. We will describe your Auto Tour in a counter clockwise direction, beginning at Port Angeles.

The park begins at the city limits with a narrow strip of land that is the starting point for Hurricane Ridge Road. The visitor center here has excellent exhibits and films on the park, but its best feature is the **Pioneer Memorial Museum**, which documents the lives and artifacts of the area's early settlers.

Olympic
National Park

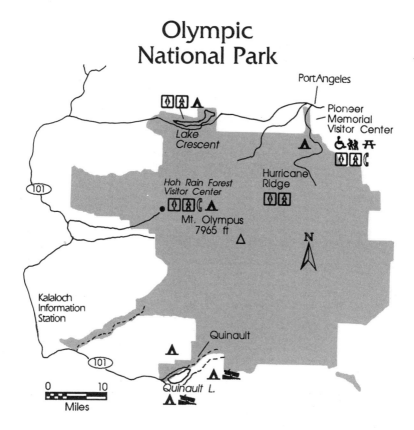

PortAngeles

Pioneer
Memorial
Visitor Center

Lake
Crescent

Hoh Rain Forest
Visitor Center

Hurricane
Ridge

Mt. Olympus
7965 ft

N

Kalaloch
Information
Station

Quinault

Quinault L.

0   10
Miles

Now you are ready to begin your drive up to **Hurricane Ridge**. The road rises sharply from the low foothills and will reach an elevation of over 5,200 feet in less than 20 miles. It is not a difficult road to drive and there are a few scenic turnouts for you to stop at and catch your breath. At Hurricane Ridge the rewards are great. From here you can look southward into the park's interior, with a view of Mount Olympus and scores of other lofty peaks, many perpetually covered with snow and ice. Looking north, you will see the ridge that you just drove up and will wonder how the car made it up. If visibility is good you will be able to see beyond Port Angeles to the Strait of Juan de Fuca, which separates the United States from Canada's Vancouver Island. On a really clear day the island will actually be visible. The unpaved road from the ridge to Deer Park is even more spectacular, but it does require experience to handle its steep grades and turns.

The mountain and sea vistas are not the only things worth seeing. The top of the ridge is a wildflower paradise. Its colors in spring and summer are brilliantly alive with white and yellow. Here, too, you will come upon attractive **Hurricane Lodge**, which contains a restaurant and other facilities (but no overnight accommodations). It has an observation deck with fine views. Several short trails originate from this point.

Now it is time to drive back down to the lowlands and head out on US 101 to your next stop, **Lake Crescent**. This large lake is 8½ miles long and, because it is over 600 feet deep, is a beautiful deep blue. And it is surrounded by mountains, which make it one of the loveliest lakes to be found anywhere. There are also some trails here (see next section).

It is about 50 miles to the next cutoff from Highway 101. This is the 17-mile drive into the **Hoh Rain Forest**. You've probably seen the Amazon Jungle in many movies, but it doesn't have anything on the Hoh Forest! Everywhere there is green. The trees and vegetation are so thick that even if it rains you won't get that wet because the forest keeps most of the rainfall from hitting the ground. What does reach you is more like a mist. At the road's end there is a visitor center and several trails which are described later.

Now work your way back to the highway, and it will take you down to the coastal section of the park, along **Ruby Beach**. This is a rugged area of seacoast and there are quite a few offshore rocks and islands to make the landscape all the more beautiful. Bathing is possible, but expect both the air and water to be chilly. Also, be aware of dangerous tides, especially near rocks. After leaving the coast area, it is less than 30 miles to the Quinnault Road. A short road here leads to another lush forest, the **Quinnault Rain Forest** at Queets. The second half of the road is unpaved, but you needn't go any further than the end of the paved portion to get the idea of what it is like.

Returning to US 101 the road continues south. At US 12, head east and it will take you back to SR 8 and then I-5 to Seattle. The US 101 loop around the park is approximately 100 miles, and the several access roads into the park and back will add on another hundred miles, so there is quite a bit of driving to do, not to mention the other activities. Therefore, you should allocate at least seven hours for the portion of the tour just described.

Getting Out/Longer Stops

There are several easy trails in addition to the short ones in the vicinity of the lodge at Hurricane Ridge. Actually, those can be extended into longer walks if you want. At Lake Crescent there is a trail about three-quarters of a mile long leading to beautiful **Marymere Falls**. Allow one hour for the round-trip. At the end of the road in the Hoh Rain Forest there are several trails, the best one being the **Hall of the Mosses**. The dense forest floor is so thick that you will not even hear your footsteps. This walk will give you a true appreciation of just what a rain forest is. Allow at least one hour.

Special Activities

In addition to **Ruby Beach**, the coastal section of Olympic Park has many nearly empty beaches. Most require a detour from US 101 at the town of Forks. Drive 14 miles to the small village of Lapush. The scenery and swimming at these beaches is excellent, but most require a good hike to reach them.

Accommodations

Since seeing the park will take you a full day or more, you will need to stay in or very near the park. A fine in-park hotel is the 52-room **Lake Crescent Lodge** (206) 962-2271, which has motel-type rooms, lodge units and cabins (B to E). It is set on the beautiful lake shore, and there are plenty of water-related activities available to guests. Four miles east, also on Lake Crescent, is the **Log Cabin Resort** (206) 928-3245, with 24 units varying from motel rooms to cabins (M). The towns of Forks and Quinnault on the western edge of the park contain some motels in the inexpensive to moderate range. For a wider choice, try the town of Port Angeles, which has many good places to stay.

Dining

All of the towns above have good places to eat. The **Lake Crescent Lodge** has a full-service restaurant and a cafeteria; the **Log Cabin Resort** has a restaurant. Additionally, if you are at **Hurricane Ridge** at lunch time, there is a good restaurant and snack bar there.

Where Do We Go From Here?

Olympic National Park is part of *Suggested Trip 8*, which includes several national parks throughout highly scenic western Washington. However, if you want an alternative, try taking the car/passenger ferry from Port Angeles to Victoria, British Columbia. There are many beautiful sights, both man-made and natural, on **Vancouver Island**. Then you can take another ferry to **Vancouver**, one of the world's most beautiful cities, before heading back south to Seattle.

30

Petrified Forest National Park

It is hard to realize that 200 million years ago this arid desert landscape was covered by a thick forest of tall coniferous trees. The passing of eons has changed all of this remarkably. It is now a multi-colored desert with petrified logs in an array of brilliant colors. The petrified trees are mostly lying on their sides and, more often than not, are broken into smaller fragments, which makes the effect even more unusual. The Petrified Forest National Park is a land of exquisite and delicate beauty. It is almost like two parks because of its two main features: the thousands of petrified logs that give it its name, as well as a large area of Arizona's fantastic Painted Desert. Each is an unforgettable sight on its own.

Facts & Figures

LOCATION/GATEWAYS/GETTING THERE: In east-central Arizona, the Petrified Forest is immediately off of I-40; in fact, there is an exit on the interstate highway right in the northern part of the park. It is less than a five-hour ride from Phoenix via interstates (I-17 and then I-40); going westbound from the city of Albuquerque it is only 4½ hours away, also by I-40.

YEAR ESTABLISHED: Originally a national monument, the Petrified Forest was designated a national park in 1962.

SIZE: 93,493 acres (or 146 square miles).

ADMISSION FEE: $5.

CLIMATE/WHEN TO GO: The dry, hot desert climate makes summer the least desirable time to visit, although because it is so dry it is tolerable. Spring and fall are delightful and the winters are quite mild, too. The park is open throughout the year, and you will find it is well-visited at all times.

ADDRESS/TELEPHONE: Superintendent, Petrified Forest National Park, AZ 86028. (602) 524-6228.

Auto Tour/Short Stops

As the park is narrow, almost all of it is easily accessible from the 27-mile road that runs through from north to south. Almost all of the major attractions are within a short walk of the paved road. You can enter from either one of two points. If traveling westbound, exit from I-40 at the park and work your way south, getting back to I-40 by going west on US 180 at the southern end of the park to Holbrook. If you are heading east, then exit at Holbrook onto US 180 and see the park going northbound, finally reaching I-40 again after completing the park. For our discussion, we will work our way south but you can simply reverse the route if coming from the other direction.

Right off the interstate is the excellent **Painted Desert Visitor Center**, which describes in detail the geologic processes that have occurred over the various periods in the earth's history and that have contributed to the formation of today's Petrified Forest. Leaving the visitor center, the road twists its way downward for a short time via a series of dramatic hairpin bends. Just as you turn southward and catch your breath from the dizzying descent, an extraordinary vista appears – the magical colors of the Painted Desert. Within a very short space there are eight overlooks with outstanding views of the desert. The best are **Kachina Point, Chinde Point, Pintado Point**, and **Lacey Point**, each as beautiful as the one preceding it. Continuing south, the Painted Desert fades away and you begin to approach the portion of the park that is filled with countless petrified logs. But first there are the remains of the 800-year-old Puerco Indian settlement, which has been partially restored. Less than a mile further along is Newspaper Rock (see next section for trail description).

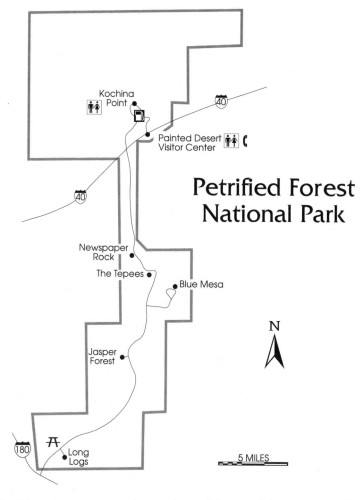

Kochina Point

Painted Desert Visitor Center

Petrified Forest National Park

Newspaper Rock

The Tepees

Blue Mesa

N

Jasper Forest

Long Logs

5 MILES

At this point you come face to face with one of the most amazing of all the sights in the park: an area known as **The Tepees**. Their shape and coloration, various layers of red, white and gray, will definitely remind you of Indian tepees but, in fact, they are large and mostly eroded mountains of clay.

Now, finally, begins the main area of petrified formations. The **Blue Mesa** is at the end of a three-mile spur off the main route. There are excellent views of various petrified objects, many having a distinct blue color. Back on the main road is **Agate Bridge**. At over 100 feet in length, it is one of the largest unbroken petrified trees in the park, and the largest visible from near the road. It is now supported by a concrete column to prevent it from breaking. This "bridge" spans a 40-foot ravine. The **Jasper Forest** and **Crystal Forest** viewpoints are next and then you will enter a portion of the park known as the Rainbow Forest. The **Long Logs** section contains the most colorful petrified logs in the entire park. Then you will reach the southern entrance station area where there is a small museum and additional exhibits about the park and local Indian cultures.

Since all of the areas above are either right on the road or a very short walk from it, the entire Auto Tour should take you no more than 2½ hours.

Getting Out/Longer Stops

Newspaper Rock, an Indian petroglyph, is near the road but requires that you descend about 120 steps. Coming back up, especially in summer, can be tiring, so take it slow. It can be seen from an overlook if you don't want to make the climb. The park service may retrict visitors to the overlook.

There is only one major trail in the park – **Giant Logs Trail** in the Rainbow Forest area. The trip covers more than three miles and takes several hours. It does not have any unusually steep grades or other difficulties, but be careful if attempting it during the summer unless you are in excellent shape. Also, make sure that you are protected from the sun and carry plenty of drinking water. All off-road hikers are required to register with park rangers, a useful precaution in this harsh land.

Many of the petrified logs are small, light, and easy to pick up. While we all like souvenirs, remember that it is against the law to remove any petrified rocks or logs from the park. Please leave everything just as you found it so tomorrow's visitor will enjoy the park as much as you did.

Accommodations & Dining

There are no overnight accommodations in the park. The nearest facilities are in Hollbrook, where several major chains are represented. Full meals are also available here; light snacks and lunches, however, can be obtained within the park.

Where Do We Go From Here?

Suggested Trip 6 includes the Petrified Forest. It is a long way from important cities so you probably wouldn't make the journey without the other attractions in that trip. However, from Phoenix a shorter trip might include the Petrified Forest, the **Monument Valley** area of Arizona and Utah, the South Rim of the **Grand Canyon** and some of the Indian ruins along I-17 toward Phoenix.

31

Rocky Mountain National Park

Rocky Mountain National Park epitomizes the grandeur of classic mountain scenery. The park contains a large segment of the Rockies Front Range – one of the most impressive collections of jagged peaks, valleys, glaciers and alpine lakes anywhere in the United States. The western face of the park has thickly forested slopes and expansive meadows, while the eastern face rises precipitously into rugged, snow-covered peaks. The "lowlands" of this park are 8,000 feet above sea level, while the highest point (Longs Peak) soars to 14,255 feet. There are some 70 peaks higher than 12,000 feet. Nowhere else in America (save for Alaska) is there such a concentration of towering peaks in so small an area. A visit to Rocky Mountain National Park is an unforgettable journey into rarefied air and breathtaking vistas.

Facts & Figures

LOCATION/GATEWAYS/GETTING THERE: It is a bit more than an hour from Denver to Estes Park in north-central Colorado, the resort community at the park's front door. US 36 is the direct route to Estes Park, although a somewhat longer detour via SR 7 provides even more scenery. After exiting the park at Grand Lake, a return trip to Denver via US 40 and I-70 will complete a loop of 250 miles. It is rare for such magnificent scenery to be found so close to a major metropolis.

YEAR ESTABLISHED: Rocky Mountain National Park was established in 1915.

SIZE: 265,229 acres (or 414 square miles).

ADMISSION FEE: $5.

CLIMATE/WHEN TO GO: The park's major road network is open from late May to late October, depending upon the amount of snowfall. Although the park is beautiful in autumn, early snows may interfere with your visit. The safest time to go is in the summer. At these altitudes the temperature is cool: sunshine is the rule, but take along a sweater or light jacket for the morning.

ADDRESS/TELEPHONE: Superintendent, Rocky Mountain National Park, Estes Park, CO 80517. (303) 586-1399.

Auto Tour/Short Stops

The park has over 300 miles of trails and is remarkably accessible and amenable to touring by car. The primary feature of any visit is the drive along **Trail Ridge Road** (US 34). About 45 miles long overall, Trail Ridge Road has a section of more than three miles at an elevation over 12,000 feet, and 11 miles above the timberline, making it the highest continuous highway in the country. The highest point on the road reaches an incredible 12,183 feet above sea level. The road contains many sharp curves, switchbacks and steep grades. It is well maintained and not overly difficult to drive, though you may not want to attempt it if you haven't had at least some previous mountain driving experience. Start out with some smaller mountains before coming to this part of Colorado!

You can enter the park either through the Estes Park or Grand Lakes sides, but we will start our description from Estes Park, as this is the preferred direction for most visitors. Just inside the entrance you will come to the **Morraine Park Visitor Center**, where you will find excellent information about the park's features and facilities. Outside, an easy half-mile nature trail will take you no more than 20 minutes. Its pleasant surroundings will introduce you to the park's varied flora and, at an 8,000-foot elevation, will help prepare you for further physical activity in these higher altitudes.

Before embarking on Trail Ridge Road, however, first take the drive down **Bear Lake Road**. En route there is fantastic scenery – high

Rocky Mountain National Park

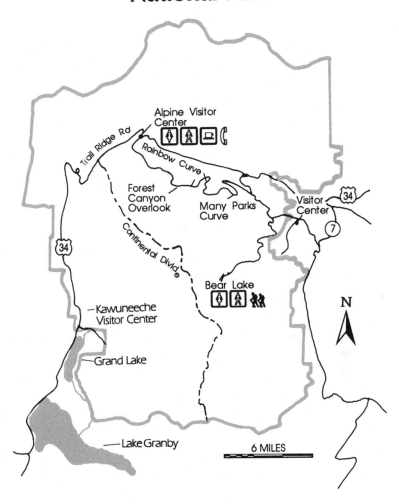

mountain peaks both near and distant, glaciers, cirques and alpine lakes. The road ends at Bear Lake. In summer try to take the shuttle bus from the parking area adjacent to the Glacier Basin camp-ground. At Bear Lake itself an unforgettable experience is the trail around the lake (see next section for a more complete description). Then make your way back to Trail Ridge Road.

The **Fall River Road** parallels a portion of Trail Ridge Road and links up with it again later on. This road is unpaved and rather difficult. Although it also provides splendid mountain vistas and access to several waterfalls, you should first do Trail Ridge Road. If this doesn't give you any trouble, you can then backtrack to the beginning of Fall River Road.

There are numerous overlooks on Trail Ridge Road, many strategically placed at the center of the road's switchbacks. This also helps widen the road at the worst turns and makes you feel less likely to slip off the mountain at any moment! The best ones are listed in the sequence that you will reach them. First is the **Many Peaks Curve**. This is followed in quick succession by **Rainbow Curve, Forest Canyon Overlook** and **Rock Cut**, where there is a spectacular and dizzying view of the forest-covered canyon floor 2,000 feet below. Opposite Rock Cut is the **Tundra Nature Trail**, a half-mile paved walk through a beautiful alpine environment. Then comes into view Lava Cliffs and shortly after that you pass the highest point on the road before coming to **Gore Range Overlook**. Then, here on top of the world, you will see a building ahead of you. This is the **Alpine Visitor Center** where there is not only information and a rest from driving but some of the very finest views in the park, either from inside the building or on the outside observation deck. Your eyes will be drawn to the snake-like outline of the road silhouetted against a backdrop of massive mountains. Similar views are available just beyond the visitor center at **Fall River Pass** and **Medicine Bow Curve**. Continuing your drive, Trail Ridge Road will then bring you through **Milner Pass**, where you will cross the Continental Divide. Then comes the last important overlook at **Fairview Curve**. From this point on the road descends along the western side of the park through Kawuneeche Valley, much more gradually than it rose at the other end. Another visitor center is located here. There isn't as much mountain scenery along this section, which is heavily wooded, but there are excellent vistas of Grand Lake (near the park's exit). You should allocate about four hours for your drive, and another hour if you decide to add on the Fall River Road.

The scenery doesn't stop once you leave the park at Grand Lake. US 40 back towards Denver passes through some spectacular mountain terrain and the drive through the **Berthoud Pass** is an amazing experience.

Getting Out/Longer Stops

Most of the trails in Rocky Mountain National Park are long (sometimes 15 miles or more) and involve steep grades. However, in addition to the previously mentioned trail at Morraine Park, and an easy half-mile trail at Sprague Lake, one that can and should be done by everyone is the half-mile circuit of **Bear Lake**. It is an easy, level walk. There is no way that the reflected image of mountain peaks in the clear, still waters of the lake can be adequately described – it simply has to be seen. If you are here at a time when there aren't too many other visitors (morning is best), you can literally hear your own heart beating. Although the trail is easy, take it slow if it is your first walk in the park – the high altitude takes some getting used to.

Special Activities

A popular way to experience some of the beauties of the park's interior is a guided **horseback ride** ($). Inquire at the Morraine Park Visitor Center.

Accommodations & Dining

There is no overnight lodging within the park. However, if you arrive the evening before, you will certainly find something to your liking in **Estes Park**, where there are more than 50 hotels. Lodging is also available at the other end of the park at **Grand Lake**, though not in the variety found at Estes Park. You can, of course, always make it back to Denver. Plenty of restaurants are to be found in the communities at either end of the park.

Where Do We Go From Here?

As any trip to Rocky Mountain National Park will likely have originated in Denver, why not take in all the sights included in *Suggested Trip 3*? If that is more than you want to accomplish on one trip, after returning to Denver head south to the many attractions in **Colorado Springs** and, just beyond that, **Canon City**, where the gorge of the Arkansas River is one of Colorado's most unusual sights.

32

Scotts Bluff National Monument

Named for a local fur trapper, Scotts Bluff National Monument was established primarily for its historic importance as a prominent landmark along the Oregon Trail for westward-bound pioneers. The escarpment, which rises 800 feet above the valley of the North Platte River (elevation above sea level is 4,649 feet), provides the most dramatic scenery in all of Nebraska. The hard sandstone (of which the escarpment is composed) has prevented it from eroding to the level of the surrounding plain. No matter which direction you approach it from, Scotts Bluff rises majestically above the surrounding terrain and is both beautiful and impressive. It is all the more so because most people know little or nothing about Scotts Bluff and, as a result, expect little.

Facts & Figures

LOCATION/GATEWAYS/GETTING THERE: In the extreme western portion of Nebraska, Scotts Bluff is five miles southwest of the town of Scottsbluff via SR 92. US 26 runs through Scottsbluff and is the primary route into the area. It is about four hours from Denver via I-25, I-80 and SR 71 to the vicinity of the monument.

YEAR ESTABLISHED: The area became a national monument in 1919.

SIZE: 3,084 acres (about five square miles).

ADMISSION FEE: $4, which includes the toll road to the summit.

CLIMATE/WHEN TO GO: The monument is open all year. The area has four distinct seasons ranging from cold winters to very hot summers with pleasant spring and fall weather. The summit road may be closed during inclement weather (mainly snow, but sometimes during summer storms, as well), so you should not plan on coming here during the winter. Any other time is appropriate for a visit.

ADDRESS/TELEPHONE: Superintendent, Scotts National Monument, P.O. Box 427, Gehring, NE 69341. (308) 436-4340.

Auto Tour/Short Stops

The monument is very small in comparison to most others in this book and there is only a single, short road. Yet, the nature of the monument still lends itself to our usual division of attractions. The road to the summit is only 1½ miles long, but it is quite a ride! Winding its way around the bluff, it passes through three tunnels and has breathtaking views on its journey to the top. No trailers are allowed on this road. Once on the summit, there are views of the fertile North Platte Valley, the town of Scottsbluff, and distant geologic features, such as Chimney Rock (23 miles away) and Laramie Peak (120 miles away). From the summit parking area there are two short trails (only six-tenths of a mile) leading to the north and south ends of the escarpment. The trails are paved, level and can be done by everyone, including the handicapped.

Before or after your ride to the top you should make a brief stop at the visitor center, which describes both the geologic and human history of the area. Near here you can walk along a portion of the original **Oregon Trail**, where some wagon ruts are still quite visible. A wagon typical of those that passed through here is on display.

Allow between one hour and 90 minutes for your visit to Scotts Bluff as described here.

Getting Out/Longer Stops

For the adventurous there is a 1½-mile trail leading from the visitor center to the top of the escarpment. It follows a different route than the road (you can not walk along the road), and does not rise as sharpl. Although it is not difficult, it still requires several hours to make the round-trip. If you want to do it, the best time would be in spring or fall. Also, you might consider driving to the top and having one person in your party drive back down while the rest of you walk, a much easier way to take the hike – much shorter, too!

Scotts Bluff National Monument

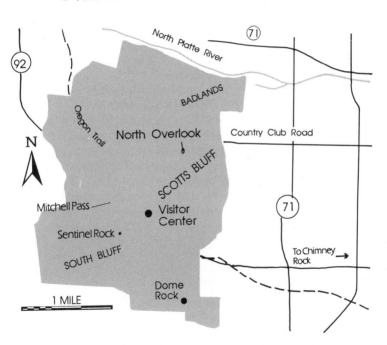

Accommodations & Dining

There are no facilities within the small monument; however, there are many hotels and restaurants in the town of Scottsbluff, with prices generally in the inexpensive range.

Where Do We Go From Here

Scotts Bluff is included as a possible extension to *Trip 2* in the last section of the book. It is not close to other attractions, but if your trip includes southern Wyoming or northeast Colorado, then Scotts Bluff is not overly out of the way. Although this is certainly not one of America's most visited national monuments (no doubt because of its location) it is a beautiful sight and would be a worthwhile addition to any of your travels.

33

Sequoia & Kings Canyon National Parks

These two huge parks are adjacent to one another at the edge of California's magnificent Sierra Nevada range. They are jointly administered and are almost always referred to collectively. The parks are home to some of the largest living things on earth – the giant sequoia trees, some of which are as much as 4,000 years old. The very largest would grow even taller were it not for the fact that their tops keep getting trimmed by bolts of lightning! But the area offers far more than these wonderful trees. The highest elevation in the contiguous United States, 14,494-foot Mount Whitney, is also here in the park. There is majestic alpine scenery throughout the park's high country and the lower elevations are graced by large forests of pine, cedar and fir trees. Although the road system, primarily consisting of the Generals Highway (which connects the two parks), does not penetrate into the high country, it does provide wonderful panoramas of the mountains and, of course, access to those huge trees.

Facts & Figures

LOCATION/GATEWAYS/GETTING THERE: Comprising a large chunk of east-central California, the parks are easily reached from SR 99. From the intersection of that road in Fresno it is only 54 miles along SR 180 to the park; from Visalia, less than 40 miles via SR 198. From San Francisco it is just under 300 miles (six hours) and from Los Angeles 225 miles (about 4½ hours).

YEAR ESTABLISHED: Sequoia became America's second national park in 1890 but, surprisingly, neighboring Kings Canyon was not given this status until 1940.

SIZE: The combined area is 864,124 acres (or 1,350 square miles). The two parks are roughly the same size.

ADMISSION FEE: $5. Entrance pass good at both parks.

CLIMATE/WHEN TO GO: Some of the roads are not open until late June or early July. Also, cooler temperatures in the higher elevations make it wise to visit during the summer or very early in the fall, before the snows set in once again.

ADDRESS/TELEPHONE: Information on both parks is available from the Superintendent, Sequoia and Kings Canyon National Parks, Three Rivers, CA 93271. (209) 565-2456. Call (204) 565-3351 for 24-hour recorded road and weather information.

Auto Tour/Short Stops

While only long hikes will physically bring you into the alpine high country, the sights from along and near the roads are spectacular enough to satisfy just about any visitor. The Generals Highway is 46 miles long and provides access to the main features of both parks. However, including one major detour and a few side roads, the total mileage in the two parks comes to about 140. You can enter from north or south, but our description here will begin from the Big Stump Entrance Station in the north.

Leave the Generals Highway and continue on with the extension of SR 180 in the direction of Cedar Grove, a one-way distance of 36 miles along the King's Canyon Highway. For now you should bypass some attractions in the beginning until you reach **Cedar Grove**. Here, the high peaks tower above the south fork of the Kings River. Spectacular views of 1,000-foot-deep Kings Canyon are available from near the road. There are several overlooks connected by either road or by short trail. These include, from west to east, **Grizzly Falls**, **Canyon View Point** and the **Grand Sentinel** before reaching **Roads End**. On the way back, the one-way **Motor Nature Trail** provides glimpses of flora and the South Fork of the Kings River. Then work your way back in the opposite direction until you arrive back at **Park Ridge** (which we skipped on the way in). Here, too, you will see the High Sierra, as well as splendid views of the valley and the distant Pacific Coast Range. A short walk from the road are several excellent vantage points from which to take in all the scenery. They include **Panorama Point, Rocking Rock, Balcony Rock, Point of View,** and **Lookout Point.** Just beyond this area is the **Grant Grove Visitor Center.** The exhibits are primarily devoted to a history of the logging industry as well as a description of early Indian inhabitants of this area.

In the **General Grant Grove,** short trails lead through the "carpeted" forest home of these giants. Almost all of them are huge, but there will be no mistaking the General Grant Tree itself, which is 267 feet high and almost 108 feet around.

Back on the Generals Highway, which has now changed to SR 198, the road twists and turns, rises and falls. It varies in elevation from 1,700 feet all the way up to a maximum of 7,643 feet at one point, so prepare for a roller-coaster ride. But back to the attractions. The **Redwood Mountain** and **Kings Canyon Overlooks** provide the best scenery on the journey immediately after leaving the Grant Grove section of the park. Next up is the **Lodgepole Visitor Center,** located on a short spur road. Here are excellent displays on the famous Sequoia trees and the geological history of the park. There are also good views of 11,204-foot Alta Peak.

A few miles south from Lodgepole is the **Giant Forest.** The main star of this grove is the **General Sherman** – the largest known Sequoia anywhere. At 275 feet high and 103 feet around, it would take 11 people standing in a circle to put their hands around the tree and it has been estimated (by people who, for some reason, figure out these things) that the tree could furnish enough lumber to make homes for 40 families.

You will soon reach a side road leading six miles to **Crystal Cave.** Well, not actually quite to the cave – from the road's end it is a half-mile by trail. Shortly after that, back on the main road is **Moro Rock,** a huge formation rising 6,000 feet above the valley. See the Getting Out section for details on both of these points of interest. Finally, not far from the south entrance is **Hospital Rock.** A short walk will take you to this formation, which bears Indian pictographs.

It will take you seven to eight hours for the complete tour as described above.

Sequoia and Kings Canyon National Parks

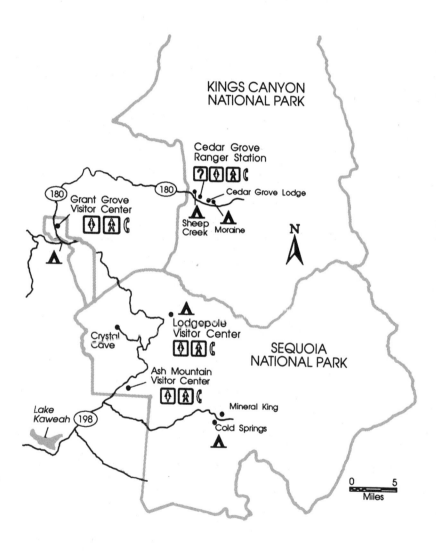

Getting Out/Longer Stops

The high country itself is accessible only to hikers and campers. While this may leave the casual visitor out, there are several other opportunities for exploring the park further.

At Crystal Cave rangers give guided tours during the summer season. They leave every half-hour from 10 in the morning until three in the afternoon. Allow about 1¼ hours for the tour and the round-trip walk (a half-mile each way) from the end of the road.

Moro Rock is plainly visible from the road, but you might want to climb to the top. It is mostly in the form of a staircase so no special skills are required. The rock rises several hundred feet from the access point, and it can be very tiring going up and fairly difficult coming back down, so be sure you are in reasonably good shape. Allow two hours for the round-trip.

Another interesting sight is **Tharp's Log**. This is actually a cabin built into a hollow log – which is a good indication of how big these Sequoias get. A one-mile trail leads to the cabin. The preceding two points of interest are both in the Giant Forest area, which contains miles and miles of mostly easy, interesting trails.

Special Activities

Sequoia and Kings Canyon contain hundreds of miles of **horse trails**. There are guided trail tours as well as horses available for rental ($). This may be the only way you will get far enough into the park to get a close look at Mount Whitney.

Accommodations

Since any proper visit to the parks will require an overnight stay, if not two nights, you should reserve well in advance and plan to stay at one of the five places within the park. These are **Cedar Grove Lodge**, an 18-room lodge in the Cedar Grove section, accessible by a rather difficult two-mile side road (E); the **Stoney Creek Lodge**, an 11-room lodge midway between Grant Grove and Giant Forest (E); or the **Grant Grove Lodge**, a 52-room facility with modest cabins, some without bath, in the Grant Grove Village (B to M). The 37-room **Montecito-Sequoia Lodge** provides modern facilities 10 miles south of Grant Grove (M-E). However, as the aforementioned are all small, you may well find yourself staying at the 245-room **Giant Forest Lodge** in the Giant Forest area. This has cabins, regular motel rooms, and some canvas-top cabins without baths that are more suited to those who usually camp out (B to E). If you can't find lodging in the park, there are several motels, most moderately-priced, in the town of Three Rivers just beyond the south entrance. For all in-park accommodations, the centralized reservation address is Sequoia Guest Services, P.O. Box 789, Three Rivers, CA 93271.

Dining

All of the hotels in the park have either a coffee shop or full-service restaurant. The **Giant Forest Lodge** is the best place for dinner as they have an excellent buffet during the summer. There is also a cafeteria for quick meals.

Where Do We Go From Here?

Sequoia and Kings Canyon Parks are part of *Suggested Trip 10*. That trip includes **Yosemite** and the proximity of the two makes it natural to see them as part of a single tour. *Trip 10* also includes many of California's other sights, both natural and man-made.

34

Shenandoah National Park

Stretching 80 miles along one of the highest sections of the famous Blue Ridge, Shenandoah National Park offers some of the most beautiful scenery east of the Mississippi. The park's elevation varies from 600 feet at the northern end to 4,050 feet at Hawksbill. The main feature of the park is the Skyline Drive, which hugs the crest of the ridge. To the west are views of the rolling Shenandoah Valley, while to the east are panoramas of fertile farmland far below the crest. The park is long and fairly narrow; but, once leaving the crest, it becomes heavily wooded. There is a great variety of tree species and the wildflowers are abundant practically all year – especially from spring through fall.

Facts & Figures

LOCATION/GATEWAYS/GETTING THERE: In northwestern Virginia, the northern entrance to the park is at Front Royal, a distance of only 60 miles from metropolitan Washington via I-66. The southern end of the park is at Waynesboro. This is 90 miles from Richmond, via I-64.

YEAR ESTABLISHED: The park was established in 1926 although it had been well explored from late Colonial times.

SIZE: 195,072 acres (or 305 square miles).

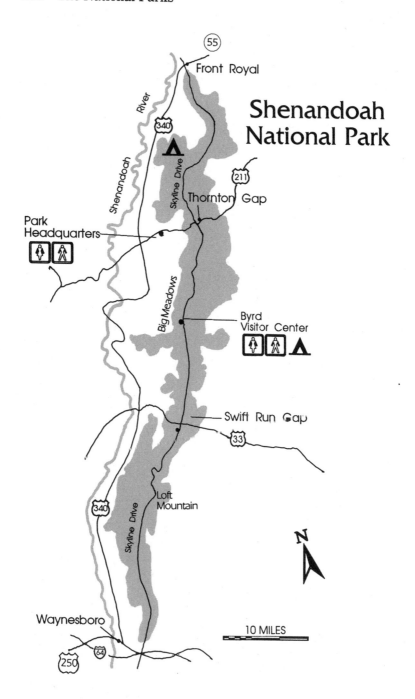

Shenandoah
National Park

Front Royal

Shenandoah River

Skyline Drive

Thornton Gap

Park
Headquarters

Big Meadows

Byrd
Visitor Center

Swift Run Gap

Loft
Mountain

Skyline Drive

Waynesboro

N

10 MILES

ADMISSION FEE: $5.

CLIMATE/WHEN TO GO: The park is open all year and the weather is good for touring during much of that time; however, many of the facilities are closed from November through March, so it is best not to go during the heart of winter. Summer is not very hot because of the high altitude. The only negative in summer is that the park can be crowded.

ADDRESS/TELEPHONE: Superintendent, Shenandoah National Park, Route 4, Box 398, Luray, VA 22835. (703) 999-2243.

Auto Tour/Short Stops

Shenandoah is one of our national parks that can be seen almost entirely by car. **Skyline Drive** runs from one end of the long and narrow park to the other, a road distance of some 105 miles. The highest elevation along the road is 3,680 feet and there are 66 scenic overlooks, more than enough to satisfy even the most avid devotee of nature's beauty. We'll describe the route's highlights from north to south, mentioning only those overlooks that are especially worthwhile.

Points of interest along Skyline Drive are well marked by numbered mileposts measured from the northern entrance at Front Royal. These numbers are indicated below for your convenience.

Very early along your drive, the **Shenandoah Valley** (milepost 2.8) and **Signal Knob Overlooks** are certainly worth a stop. The road climbs gently in the beginning until it levels out and remains at about 3,000 feet. There are no steep grades or severe switchbacks on the road. Between the first two vistas will come the **Dickey Ridge Visitor Center** (4.6), where you can obtain information on the park. Right after that there is the lovely, though unfortunately-named, **Hogback Overlook** (21), which offers views of the twisting Shenandoah River.

One of the main attractions of Skyline Drive is its passage through **Mary's Rock Tunnel** (32.4), a distance of about 700 feet. An excellent overlook at the tunnel's south entrance provides a great view of the surrounding terrain.

Then comes the **Pinnacles Overlook** (36.7), followed by **Crescent Rock** (44.4), which affords the best view of Hawksbill, Shenandoah

Park's highest peak. Soon after this you reach the **Harry Byrd Visitor Center** (51.2), where various exhibits document both the history of the park and the culture of the surrounding area.

South of the visitor center are two more grand vistas, **Rockytop** (78.2) and **Big Run** (81.1). At that point you reach the end of the Skyline Drive and the park's exit.

Allow 3 to 3½ hours for traversing the Skyline Drive with stops at the viewpoints.

Getting Out/Longer Stops

There are ample opportunities to extend your visit with some of the trails that begin along Skyline Drive. Remember, however, that all of the trails lead down from the narrow crest on which the road lies. As a result, each one requires a return climb. Among the best trails are **Little Stoney Man** (39.1), a 1½-mile round-trip which provides some of the best views of the valley from anywhere in the park. Allow 1½-2 hours for this trail. The **Whiteoak Canyon Trail** (42.6) leads to a beautiful falls, but it is a half-day, five-mile trek. There is also a trail leading to the summit of Hawksbill. This is two miles round-trip and takes less than two hours to complete. The **Dark Hollow Falls Trail** (50.9) leads to a beautiful waterfall by that name. It is 1½ mileslong and can be accomplished in under 90 minutes. Guides and maps to all of the trails can be found at the visitor centers. Several nature trails at Dickey Ridge, Matthew's Arm, Skyland, Big Meadow, and Loft Mountain do not descend beneath the crest. Finally, almost 100 miles of the **Appalachian Trail** traverses the park. Access to it is easy from many of the parking areas along Skyline Drive.

Special Activities

Horseback riding is available for either hourly periods or half-day trips ($). Inquire either at Skylands or Big Meadows.

Accommodations

Within the park boundaries is **Skyland Lodge**, a 186-room motor inn with some cottages. This attractive facility is in a beautiful setting with panoramic views on all sides (M). In-park reservations are through ARA Services, (800) 999-4714. Varied accommodations are available at both ends of the park (the towns of Front Royal and Waynesboro) and west of the park in Luray and Harrisonburg. The latter are accessible from routes that cross Skyline Drive at Thornton Gap and Swift Run Gap.

Dining

The best eating place in the park is **Skyland Lodge**. Other restaurants can be found in all the towns bordering on the park's several entrances.

Where Do We Go From Here?

Suggested Trip 1 includes Shenandoah National Park, continuing with the **Blue Ridge Parkway**, which begins where Skyline Drive ends. However, if that trip is not to your liking, the scenic eastern highlands of West Virginia are nearby. Also, **Luray Caverns** is but a few miles west of the park and should be seen as part of any visit to Shenandoah. For those who want to combine cities and history with the scenery, a circle route of Virginia and the Washington, D.C. area is recommended.

35

Yellowstone
National Park

America's first national park is also one of its largest – the largest in the 48 contiguous states – and the only one that extends over three different states. Although parts of the park are in Montana and Idaho, most of the park's area and all of its major attractions are in Wyoming. Yellowstone Park is a broad volcanic plateau that generally lies between 7,000 and 8,500 feet above sea level, with peaks that rise 2,000-4,000 feet above the plateau. That dry geologic description hardly begins to do the park justice, but no words really can.

Probably the most famous single feature of Yellowstone is Old Faithful. As beautiful as it is, by the time you have finished seeing Yellowstone you will most likely rank it as one of the lesser attractions in the park. Yellowstone is a microcosm of America's natural beauty – its variety is unsurpassed by any other national park. Besides the geysers, geothermal activity has produced gurgling mudpots and colorful algae-containing waters from the hot earth that simply defy description. Then, too, there are elegant mountains, deep canyons, high rushing waterfalls and rivers, forests, and lakes. There is something for everyone – so much so that you will be hard-pressed to remember it all once you have left.

The devastating fire of 1988 is history. Although the damage was extensive, it never affected the areas seen by visitors to the extent that the media would have had you believe. Regardless, the past eight years are a tribute to the healing power of nature.

Facts & Figures

LOCATION/GATEWAYS/GETTING THERE: There are five entrances to Yellowstone National Park, which is in the northwestern corner of Wyoming, with narrow strips extending across the border into neighboring states. From the south (and Grand Teton National Park), US 89/191/287 is the only approach. The two access routes from the east are US 14/16/20 from Cody, Wyoming and US 212 from Red Lodge, Montana. The northern access is via US 89 from Livingston, Montana while the western approach is US 20 from Idaho Falls. The nearest significant commercial airport is three hours away in Bozeman, Montana, while Salt Lake City is seven hours away. You can also fly into Jackson, Wyoming if you don't want to drive that far to reach the park.

YEAR ESTABLISHED: America's original national park, Yellowstone was given this designation by Congress in 1872.

SIZE: Three times as large as Rhode Island, Yellowstone covers 2,211,823 acres (or 3,468 square miles).

ADMISSION FEE: $10. Passes from Yellowstone are also valid at Grand Teton National Park.

CLIMATE/WHEN TO GO: Most roads are open from the beginning of May until the end of October, but there are limited facilities after the early part of September. Since the summer is dry and pleasant (mornings are often quite chilly), June, July and August are the best times to see the park, especially for an initial visit. Yellowstone, however, has special wonders reserved for every season of the year.

ADDRESS/TELEPHONE: Superintendent, Yellowstone National Park, P.O. Box 168, Yellowstone Park, WY 82190. (307) 344-7381. When in the park you can get up-to-the-minute information by tuning your AM car radio to 1606 KHz.

Auto Tour/Short Stops

Considering the immensity of this state-sized park, Yellowstone is remarkably easy to see by car. The **Grand Loop Road**, which circles the central plateau area, touches or comes very near to almost every major attraction. This road covers nearly 150 miles and, with access roads to and from your entrance and exit points, plan on covering close to 250 total miles within the park itself. Therefore, in addition to time for seeing the various areas mentioned below, allow close to seven hours for travel time alone, because you can't go fast on these roads. Besides the fact that you want to take in the scenery, traffic in the summer months is often very heavy, sometimes causing considerable delays.

Yellowstone National Park

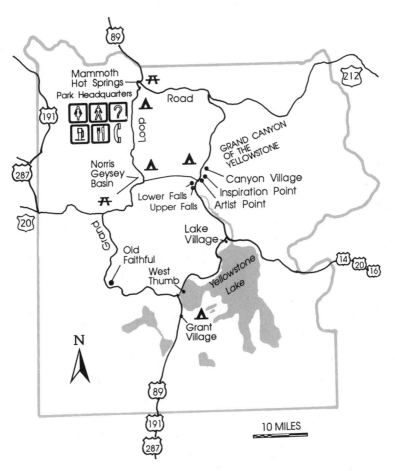

As the road is a complete loop it doesn't matter which park entrance you use or where you start the tour. For purposes of this discussion, we will begin from the park headquarters at **Mammoth Hot Springs**. Mammoth Hot Springs, in addition to the administrative offices of the park, has the **Mammoth Visitor Center**, which can provide information on the natural and human history of the park. There are six other visitor centers and/or museums in Yellowstone, which will be addressed as we travel through the park.

The main features of Mammoth Hot Springs are the multicolored terraces – limestone formations being affected by geothermal forces. The area is both stunning and eerie. Easy walking is provided by way of boardwalks. A word of caution is in order here: wherever you see boardwalks in the park, stay on them; the surrounding terrain is often hot and the crust may be very soft. You can see everything worth seeing from the designated routes. Some of the major formations in the terrace area are the **Liberty Cap, Devil's Thumb, Cleopatra's Terrace** and **Minerva Terrace**. After you complete the trail, a short one-way auto loop covers the **Upper** or **White Elephant Back Terrace**. Allow at least an hour to visit the Mammoth Hot Springs area.

Proceeding south on the Grand Loop Road past the glass-like **Obsidian Cliffs**, your next stop along this other-worldly journey is the **Norris Geyser Basin**. Just a few steps from the parking area is the **Norris Museum**, which explains the geology of the area. To the left of the museum is the **Back Basin Trail**. Walking this trail will take you by some 27 different geysers and, unless you are very unlucky, one or more of them will be erupting during your visit. The predicted eruption times can be found posted at the museum. Then return to the museum and begin the boardwalk trail to the right of the building. This is the **Porcelain Basin Trail** and it contains many other beautiful examples of the more than 10,000 geysers in the park. But more important here are the exquisite colors of the ground. They are caused by algae growing in the warm water that combines with soft minerals on the surface. It looks as if a giant artist spilled his palate on the ground. Allow about 90 minutes to two hours for the two basins and the museum, excluding any time you have to spend waiting for a geyser to put on its show. There are benches or logs to sit on at most of the larger geysers while you're waiting for an eruption.

Continuing our Grand Loop tour, the next stop is in Madison, where the **Madison Explorers Museum** has interesting exhibits on the park's earliest visitors. You will then pass by the **Firehole Falls** and continue your drive to the Firehole River before arriving at the **Lower** and **Midway Geyser Basins**. The key features here are the colorful "paintpots" and "mud volcanoes," where strange gurgling sounds and strong aromas emanate from the earth. Both children and adults will delight in them all. You will also see numerous places where steaming hot water runs into the Firehole River and so understand where it gets its name. Thirty to 45 minutes should be adequate for this area.

Just a few miles further ahead is Old Faithful Village. There is a visitor center here and just outside the building is the best area for viewing eruptions of **Old Faithful** (which occur approximately every hour and last from two to five minutes). The next predicted eruption will be posted at the visitor center, although you can usually tell when it is due to go off by the huge crowd that has gobbled up the best places to watch. Moral of the story: be there early. A trail in this area also leads to such other sights as the **Giant Geyser** (whose eruption schedule will also be on display). Allow a one-hour minimum for this trail.

About 15 miles past Old Faithful, the Grand Loop Road reaches the junction with the Rockefeller Parkway and your route will turn to the north. Now you will be riding along the edge of huge Yellowstone Lake. Just before getting to Lake Junction there is a short spur road leading to **Natural Bridge**, a 10-minute walk. It is worth the time to see this huge formation set in a forested canyon. At **Lake Village** are magnificent views of the blue lake with mountain backdrops. There is another short trail that leads through more thermal areas. The lake provides an interesting backdrop to these features. A visitor center with information about the lake is also here. Allow 30 minutes for exploring the lake area.

Sixteen miles north of Fishing Bridge Junction, the Grand Loop Road will bring you to the remarkable Canyon area. A spur road leads along the South Rim of the **Grand Canyon of the Yellowstone River**. The spectacular coloring, especially the golden and yellowish hues of the rock, combined with the deep canyon and the rushing waterfalls make this not only one of the most beautiful sights in the park, but in all the world. Be sure to walk from the south rim road to see the views from **Artist Point**.

Then, just over the bridge that connects the two sides of the canyon, you will be at **Canyon Village**. After stopping at the Canyon Visitor Center take the one-way road leading along the north rim. **Red Rock, Lookout Point, Grand View Point** and last, but not least,

Inspiration Point are the must-see features here. From Lookout Point the views of the over 300-foot Lower Falls (twice as high as Niagara) and the 109-foot Upper Falls are fantastic. At least 1½ hours should be allowed for the canyon area.

Continuing north, the terrain becomes more mountainous as you pass **Mount Washburn** (10,324 feet). At Tower Junction, head westward for the final leg of the Grand Loop back to Mammoth Hot Springs. Although there are no unusual features along this stretch, the overall scenery is quite beautiful; this is especially true once the road descends and Mammoth Hot Springs comes into view.

Getting Out/Longer Stops

The suggested tour includes many fabulous views of the Canyon area, but you can also choose to walk along the Grand Canyon of the Yellowstone's north and south rims instead of taking your car from one observation point to another. Add about one hour for each rim you explore. Of course, there are longer trails heading into the back-country in most sections of the park. Some are relatively easy. You can secure information on these at any visitor center.

Special Activities

The sights can be seen by **horseback** ($). There are several areas where horses can be rented and the trail system is extensive. On Yellowstone Lake you can rent **motorboats, launches** or **rowboats** for a leisurely break from other forms of sightseeing. Multi-day guided tours of the park are also an option but, since the park is so easy to see from the Grand Loop, this rather expensive option is not going to gain you very much.

Accommodations

Because the park is so vast and the points of interest almost uncountable, you will have to spend an absolute minimum of one night inside the park. Six facilities within the park provide accommodations of all types. As there are more places to stay in Yellowstone than in just about any other national park, we'll put them into list form for ease of reading.

Canyon Village: Hotels and cabins (588 total units), located in Canyon Junction (M).

Lake Lodge and Cabins: Hotel and cabins (186 units) at Lake Junction (M to E).

Lake Yellowstone Hotel and Cabins: Hotel and cabins (292 units) at Lake Junction (B to E).

Mammoth Hot Springs Hotel: Hotel and cabins (226 units), in the park headquarters area (B to E).

Old Faithful Inn: Lodge rooms (325 units), no elevator, opposite the Old Faithful Geyser (B to E).

Grant Village: Motor inn (296 units), located at Grant Village (M).

All of these hotels are rather old but many have been extensively renovated. Don't be fooled by the fact they total almost 2,000 rooms – they fill up fast in summer. You should reserve early through the centralized reservation service. Write to the Travel Director, TW Recreational Services, Inc., Yellowstone National Park, WY 82190 or call (307) 244-7456. Abundant motel-style accommodations are also available in the communities near most entrances of the park. Specifically, they can be found in the towns between the east entrance and Cody, Wyoming and in Cook City, Gardiner, Silver Gate and, especially, West Yellowstone, Montana.

Dining

Every hotel in the park has a full-service restaurant (with the exception of Lake Lodge & Cabins, which has only a cafeteria). Several have a coffee shop and/or cafeteria in addition to the dining room. Food service is generally quite good.

Where Do We Go From Here?

Yellowstone is included in *Suggested Trip 5*. If, however, your time is limited and you cannot cover everything in that trip, you should at least combine Yellowstone with **Grand Teton National Park**, since they are neighbors. Salt Lake City is a good starting point for a loop using this more limited itinerary. Another alternative to *Trip 5* is a circle tour of the state of Wyoming. This will involve about as much mileage as *Trip 5* but, besides Yellowstone and Grand Teton, can include entirely different sights. Some of the routes across northern Wyoming from or to Yellowstone are absolutely spectacular.

36

Yosemite National Park

Yosemite is justifiably one of America's most famous and popular parks; its spectacular scenery is sure to impress even those who have seen practically every other park. On the western slopes of the Sierra Nevada mountains, Yosemite encompasses a staggering array of sights – majestic peaks, sheer granite walls, the well-known domes and pinnacles, immense waterfalls, rushing rivers, huge trees, forests and more.

To most visitors, Yosemite National Park refers to a small but dramatic area known as Yosemite Valley. This, however, represents only 0.5% of the park's total area! The other, far bigger portion has enough to make the visit worthwhile even if Yosemite Valley did not exist. Only Yellowstone and possibly Olympic National Park have a greater variety of sights.

Facts & Figures

LOCATION/GATEWAYS/GETTING THERE: Yosemite National Park, in north-central California, is only a four-hour drive from San Francisco. The major approach road from the bay area (and also from Sacramento) is SR 120. SR 140 is another access route from San Francisco or from the central California coastal region. SR 41 from Fresno is the major approach from the south. From Reno, Nevada, the park can be reached via US 395 to SR 120 westbound. The most direct route to SR 120 from San Francisco is I-580 and then I-205 directly to SR 120.

Yosemite National Park

Plute Mt.
10,541 Ft.

Lake Eleanor

(120)

Hetch Hetchy Res.

Tioga Road

Toulumne
Meadows
Visitor Center

Big Oak Flat
Entrance

Yosemite Falls

Valley Visitor Center

El Capitan
7569 Ft.

Yosemite Valley

Glacier Point

Arch Rock Entrance

(140)

Glacier Point Rd

Wawona Rd.

Mariposa Grove

0   10

Miles

YEAR ESTABLISHED: Designated a state reserve in 1864, Yosemite became the nation's second national park in 1890.

SIZE: 761,150 acres (or 1,189 square miles).

ADMISSION FEE: $5.

CLIMATE/WHEN TO GO: A summer visitor in Yosemite will find the weather very pleasant; fall and spring are also nice but, at the higher elevations, can be cold. One of the most important attractions, Yosemite's majestic waterfalls, tend to dry up by late summer. They are at their peak in May and June, but sometimes in May sections of the park will remain inaccessible if there have been heavy winter snows. Though the park will be crowded, I suggest you plan your trip for the second half of June or the first half of July at the very latest.

ADDRESS/TELEPHONE: Superintendent, Yosemite National Park, P.O. Box 577, Yosemite National Park, CA 95389. (209) 372-0200.

Auto Tour/Getting Out

Because of traffic restrictions, most portions of Yosemite do not lend themselves to the kind of Auto Tour that served us so well in other parks. Secondly, in some ways Yosemite is almost like three parks in one. Our description will be geared to touring in these three distinctive sections: Yosemite Valley; the southern (Mariposa Grove) portion; and the northern (Tuolumne) section.

The park's popularity has led to big traffic problems. Private vehicles may be prohibited from certain areas at times to relieve congestion. One good option is to leave your car in the huge parking facility at Curry Village. From here you can take convenient and frequent shuttles throughout the valley or, even better, walk!

Yosemite Valley

This is the most beautiful and dramatic part of the park and it is also the easiest to visit. The valley is approximately seven miles long and has an average width of only three-quarters of a mile. The Merced River flows through the valley, which is famous for its waterfalls and the sheer walls that almost completely envelope it. These walls often rise more than 3,000 feet above the valley floor.

Seeing the valley is easy because it is extremely flat – you can walk along it as you would along a street in your home town. Roads are generally one-way (the south side road is eastbound and the north side is westbound), but travel in private vehicles is severely restricted and all but prohibited in the easternmost section of the valley. This is not a problem, however, because there is frequent shuttle service within the valley and you can get off wherever you like. Drivers announce points of interest so you know exactly where to get off.

Yosemite Falls is truly an awesome sight. The Upper Falls drop an unbelievable 1,430 feet in one fell swoop, while the Lower Falls plunge another 320. Including some smaller intervening cascades, the total drop is 2,425 feet, almost half a mile. (Imagine, if you will, water dropping from the top of two World Trade Centers piled on top of one another – that is roughly the distance involved.) The valley has several other major waterfalls ranging in height from 317 feet to 1,612 feet. The ones that you should see close up are **Vernal Falls, Illilouette Falls, Nevada Falls, Bridalveil Falls** and **Ribbon Falls**. Short trails lead from the road to each of them and, believe me, you won't get tired of seeing so many.

The walls of the valley (its domes and pinnacles, to use the proper terms) are just as famous as the waterfalls. The best known is, of course, **El Capitan**, whose smooth surface rises 3,600 feet and is so close to the road that you can easily walk up and touch it. (Many people also climb El Capitan!) Other significant similar features are **Half Dome, North Dome, Cathedral Spires** and the **Three Brothers**. They are all easy to spot and a visit to the valley isn't complete unless you've seen them all.

Yosemite is also home to **Mirror Lake** in the easternmost portion of the valley. The shuttle bus ends a bit before reaching this point, but it is a short walk and you will not be disappointed with the staggeringly beautiful image of the nearby mountain peaks reflected in the lake.

Finally, the park's primary visitor center is also in the valley and here you will find plenty of information about the park. It is also where many of the special activities originate (see appropriate section). Allow at least five hours for exploring the valley.

South (Mariposa Grove) Area

Now its time to get into your car. Leaving the valley you will pick up SR 41. Before passing through the Wawona Tunnel at the west end of the valley, stop at the east portal for a breathtaking panorama back into the valley you have just left. Then SR 41 heads down toward the Wawona Village area. Just before the south entrance station, there is a spur road which goes into the Mariposa Grove. Here you will find dozens of giant sequoia trees, the biggest being the huge **Grizzly Giant** with a girth of almost 97 feet and a height of 210 feet. There are taller specimens here but none are as immense overall.

Returning towards the valley now (or on the way down to Mariposa if you will be leaving the park after visiting the Grove), turn off on **Glacier Point Road**, generally open June to October only. This road climbs gently at first through heavily forested areas until it suddenly and dramatically rises in a series of looping turns, bringing you to **Glacier Point**. Here is probably the single most spectacular view of the entire park. The view of Half Dome and the distant Sierra Nevada peaks is one you will never forget. Looking straight down you can see Yosemite Valley beneath you. Details such as roads and buildings, looking like toys, are readily discernible. Yet, even though it seems to be at your feet, the distance back to Yosemite Valley by road is 30 miles over the narrow, circuitous roads.

Allow at least five hours for your trip to Mariposa Grove and Glacier Point if you are returning to the valley, or about four if you will be leaving the park at the south entrance.

North (Tuolumne) Area

Only a small percentage of visitors to Yosemite see this part of the park, so there are no major traffic problems here. The Tioga Pass Road crosses this section from east to west. Unless you are headed to Reno you will have to turn around and come back when you reach the eastern terminus of the park near the town of Lee Vining. Unfortunately, the drive is rather long and difficult and has many steep grades and sharp turns. But the mountain scenery is exceptionally rewarding for those who undertake the trip, with mountain meadows, canyons and peaks to be seen. Most people who tour this section use it as the starting point for trips into the back-country, for this is where most of the trail heads leading into the wilderness are found. There are a number of pullouts, however, for those who simply want to drive along the Tioga Pass Road and take in the scenery. The major attraction along this road is **Tuolumne Meadow**, Yosemite's largest meadow where the abundant wild flowers are at their most spectacular in early summer. A small visitor center is also located here. Also of interest is the **Tioga Pass**, where the road reaches the crest of the Sierra Nevada at an elevation of 9,945 feet. Tenaya Lake, one of several bodies of water visible from the Tioga Road, is Yosemite's largest and one of its most beautiful lakes. Should you opt for this drive, allow a half-day if you will be exiting at Lee Vining, or a full day if you intend to return to Yosemite Village.

Special Activities

There is a two-hour guided tour of the valley in an **open-air tram** for those that do not want to use the shuttle bus ($). I will mention, however, that the bus is a better way to see the sights since it allows you to get off and on at will. That way you can walk right up to the waterfalls and other features, then get back on the shuttle whenever you are ready.

For those not wishing to drive down to Mariposa Grove and Glacier Point, there is an all-day **bus tour** that covers these two places well ($). The disadvantage is that the pace is slow, with an extended lunch break, so you can probably make more effective use of the time on your own. The tour is a good choice, however, if you do not like driving on precipitous mountain roads, which the drive southbound will require. If you take the bus you can keep your eyes closed until you get to your destination. (I heard that the tour bus drivers sometimes keep their eyes closed too!)

If you have a lot of time available, a lovely side trip can be made from the Big Oak Flat Entrance, via Evergreen Road to Yosemite's **Hetch Hetchy** area. The road extends about 11 miles from Big Oak Flat. This area is mainly an access point for adventurers seeking out the vast wilderness of Yosemite's north. However, you can come here just for the unforgettable view of the Hetch Hetchy Reservoir nestled in the High Sierra and the Tuolumne River traversing a narrow gorge.

Finally, of course, **horseback riding** is available for the more adventurous visitor. Ask at any visitor center.

Accommodations

Yosemite is one of those parks where the size and number of activities will require that you spend at least one night in the park. Most lodging is located in the valley. There is the famous **Ahwahnee Hotel** (121 lodge-type rooms), with an elegant and refined atmosphere (E). The **Yosemite Lodge** has 495 units varying from hotel rooms to cabins, some of which have no bath (M to E). **Curry Village** features 625 modest cabins or cottages, as well as tent cabins (M). Outside of the valley is the **Wawona Hotel**, a stately 75-room lodge eight miles north of the Mariposa Grove (E). **The Redwoods** is a 78-unit complex of cottage apartments and studios (E). It is six miles north of the southern entrance to the park. There is no restaurant here, but all units have kitchen facilities.

The town of El Portal, just outside the park's valley section, also has a selection of motels.

Reservations for all in-park lodging should be made early, especially if you are visiting at the height of the season, through Yosemite Concession Services Corporation, (209) 252-4848 or 372-1000.

Dining

Elegant, formal dining is available at the Ahwahnee. There is also an attractive restaurant at the **Wawona Hotel**. The **Yosemite Lodge** has a restaurant, coffee shop and cafeteria, while **Curry Village** offers only a cafeteria.

Where Do We Go From Here?

Trip 10 incorporates Yosemite with numerous other California attractions. An interesting alternate routing from San Francisco takes in the **San Francisco Bay** area, **Yosemite**, including the Tuolumne section, and then on to **Reno** and beautiful **Lake Tahoe**. If you want to make the trip a loop, return to San Francisco via I-80.

37

Zion National Park

A rugged, lush and narrow canyon with a sometimes raging river and spectacularly colored rocky promontories characterize Zion Canyon, which has been compared by many to the Valley of Yosemite. The sheer rock walls are indeed similar, but those at Zion have far more color. The canyon road extends eight miles through canyons, past buttes and mesas, interspersed with vegetation. The canyon itself narrows from half a mile in width at the beginning to just 300 feet at the end!

Zion's mountains are famous for their color – brownish red at the bottom, becoming whiter as they rise toward the sky. Then, too, there are fantastic shades of purple and lilac, all the more brilliant when captured in the sunlight.

The fanciful names of many of the park's features probably owe their origin to early Mormon settlers. But when you see the dramatic formations that gave rise to these names you will fully understand the awe that must have been felt by these early visitors.

Facts & Figures

LOCATION/GATEWAYS/GETTING THERE: In the southwestern corner of Utah's Color Country, the entrance is on SR 9, which connects to I-15 near St. George on the west and with US 89 (access to Bryce) on the east. SR 9 is referred to as the Zion-Mount Carmel Highway and a portion of it forms an integral part of the park's road network.

YEAR ESTABLISHED: Seen by white men as early as 1776, the area was more fully explored in the 1870s. Zion became a national park in 1919, but did not take its current form until the completion of the Zion-Mount Carmel Highway in 1930.

SIZE: 146,551 acres (or 229 square miles).

ADMISSION FEE: $5.

CLIMATE/WHEN TO GO: In southern Utah, Zion's summers are very hot, especially on the canyon floor. Spring and fall are better times to visit, when temperatures are moderate. The park is open in winter and can be quite beautiful when covered with snow. But the snow can sometimes be heavy enough to close portions of the road network, so stick to other seasons if you can.

ADDRESS/TELEPHONE: Superintendent, Zion National Park, Springdale, UT 84767. (801) 772-3256.

Auto Tour/Short Stops

The narrowness of the canyon makes it easy to explore Zion with your car, but there is ample opportunity for stretching your legs as well. We will assume that you will be arriving from the east (US 89), as many people do because this is the route from Bryce Canyon. Total driving within the park, including the canyon road, the Zion-Mount Carmel Highway and some short spurs is only about 24 miles. Even if you come from the west and double back on the Zion-Mount Carmel Highway, the total distance is a modest 35 miles within the main section of the park.

The Zion-Mount Carmel Highway section, though not in the canyon, is one of great beauty. The road itself, considered an engineering marvel when built, is still quite wonderful, with its constant zig-zagging and climbing. Despite this, it is fairly easy to drive. Shortly after entering the park you should stop at the **Checkerboard Mesa**, an unusual sloping, whitish-gray formation with thin lines criss-crossing it like a giant checkerboard. You pass through a short tunnel afterwards and then approach the second, and longer, Zion Tunnel. Before entering the tunnel stop at the turn-out to view Zion Canyon from the overlook (see next section for trail information). The tunnel itself is well over a mile long. Inside there are several openings, or "windows," that look out into the canyon. When the road first opened you were allowed to stop and get out to take a better look, but this practice has been stopped because the number of visitors would make stopping in the tunnel dangerous.

After emerging from the tunnel, the highway begins a series of six dizzying switchbacks. You won't know if you should keep your eye on the road or the fantastic scenery as you literally drop into the canyon. I suggest you keep your eye on the road, but stop at the parking area amid the switchbacks to take in the amazing glory of nature that surrounds you. This portion of the highway ends at the junction with the canyon road, or Zion Canyon Scenic Drive. Before heading up the canyon, take a short detour south (turn left) to visit the **Zion Visitor Center**. Besides exhibits and information, there is an excellent view of the two peaks called the Towers of the Virgin and of the canyon itself.

Now you can begin the drive into the main canyon. Some of the formations you will pass (and there are plenty of pull outs along the road so that you can stop and get a firsthand look) are the **East Temple, Twin Brothers, Mountain of the Sun**, the **Altar of Sacri-**

fice, the **Beehives** and the **Sentinel**. These come upon you in quick succession (the entire canyon road is not that long). A bit further along will be the Court of the Patriarchs, which includes the **Three Patriarchs**, **Lady Mountain** and **Castle Dome**. Just beyond this point you will reach the **Great White Throne**, one of Zion's most famous landmarks and an excellent example of the layers of color for which Zion's peaks are known.

Shortly after you pass the Great White Throne, the road ends at the **Temple of Sinawana**, a huge natural amphitheater. Two large stone objects in the middle of the amphitheater are called the Altar and the Pulpit. The Temple of Sinawana is the beginning of the Gateway to the Narrows (see next section). When finished here, head back down the canyon. Before leaving the park you will see the **Watchman**, a vast mountain that guards the southern end of the park. Allow about three hours for the driving portion of your visit.

Getting Out/Longer Stops

Although the scenery from the car and overlooks is wonderful, there are several opportunities for easy walks that will add considerably to your enjoyment of the park.

The **Canyon Overlook Trail** (at the east entrance of the Zion Tunnel) covers about one mile and can be done in an hour. It is an easy walk with spectacular views of the canyon from above. All the other trails are at the bottom of the canyon.

Two popular trails within the canyon are **Weeping Rock** and the **Gateway to the Narrows**. The first is a simple half-hour nature trail. The latter is about a mile one way and requires 1½ hours for the round-trip. Leading from the Temple of Sinawana, it ends at the Narrows itself. Only a couple of hundred feet wide, the area is between towering cliffs; the Virgin River is at your feet and water dripping down the canyon walls has caused vegetation to grow from the walls in many places. It is a worthwhile experience. At the end you can peer into the Narrows, one of the narrowest canyons to be found anywhere. The Narrows itself extends more than 10 miles and hiking within it should not be attempted by the casual visitor. It and many other long trails in the park can be quite difficult.

Special Activities

At Zion Lodge (about half-way through the canyon) you can arrange for **open-air tram** or **bus tours** of the canyon as well as **horseback riding** ($).

Note: The park's northwestern section, called the **Kolob Canyon**, is not accessible by road from the main portion of the park. Not visited by many people, it can be reached from I-15 and is a distance of about 45 miles from the park's main entrance station on SR 9. If you opt to see this section you will view the **Finger Canyons**, an area of tall red spires somewhat reminiscent of Bryce. The six-mile road off of I-15 has several good overlooks and there is also a small visitor center here which explains the geology of this portion of the park.

Accommodations

Excellent accommodations are available inside the park at **Zion Lodge**, which has 120 lodge rooms and cabins (E). Contact TW Recreational Services, (801) 586-7686. In addition, the town of Springdale, just outside the park's main entrance, has almost a dozen motels to choose from.

Dining

Zion Lodge has an excellent restaurant as well as a coffee shop for snacks and lighter meals. There are also several good restaurants in Springdale.

Where Do We Go From Here?

Zion is included in *Trip 7* in the section which follows this chapter. For shorter trips, Zion is often included in a loop from Las Vegas, passing through **Bryce Canyon National Park** and including the North Rim of the **Grand Canyon**.

Suggested Trips

This section suggests tours that combine visits to the parks with other attractions nearby. All of these trips assume that you will either be driving from your home city to a gateway or flying to a gateway city and renting a car. The mileage and time allotment shown is from the gateway, so that if you are driving from another location, both the mileage and days should be adjusted upward accordingly. All of the trips return to the same location as they began, but can be reworked into one-way itineraries. While this can often save a lot of mileage and time on a fly-drive vacation, remember that one-way car rentals (when they are possible) are significantly higher in cost and often include exorbitant drop-off charges. It can also be difficult to get discounted airfares on flights that are not round-trips to and from the same city. Refer back to the chapter on each park for more detail. The itineraries are merely suggestions, not fixed plans, and can easily be tailored to fit your individual tastes.

The schedule for the first and last day of each trip makes another assumption – that you are flying to and from the gateway and time to do this is built in. Therefore, the itinerary may seem sparse for the first day, because it allows time for a mid-day arrival, and the last day, so that you can return the car and catch a mid-afternoon flight. Even if the scheduled arrival would allow plenty of time for sightseeing or travel, you never know when there will be delays en route, especially if your flight plans call for a change of planes. If you are driving from your home and want to use the itineraries "as is," then plan to arrive at the gateway near the time I have suggested.

Trip 1

Along the Blue Ridge

PARK HIGHLIGHTS: Great Smoky Mountains National Park (North Carolina/Tennessee); Shenandoah National Park (Virginia). Optional Extension to Mammoth Cave National Park (Kentucky).

GATEWAY: Knoxville, Tennessee

ESTIMATED MILES: 1,170 (1,750 with extension)

TIME: 9 days (14 with extension)

FIRST DAY: Leaving Knoxville, take I-40 eastbound to I-81, northbound. I-81 will be the primary artery on the northbound leg of this trip. It is quite scenic as it parallels the Appalachian Mountain area that will comprise the bulk of your sightseeing as you travel southbound later on. You'll arrive in **Bristol** on the Virginia-Tennessee border late in the afternoon and have time to explore this historic community.

SECOND DAY: The interstate will speed you far into Virginia, arriving at **Natural Bridge** in just under three hours of pleasant driving. Natural Bridge rises 215-feet above the creek which it spans and is an interesting short walk from the parking area just off the highway. A short distance ahead, also off I-81, is the town of **Lexington**, with numerous attractions dating from the Civil War era, including the renowned **Virginia Military Institution**, the **Stonewall Jackson House**, and the impressive chapel to Robert E. Lee on the campus of **Washington and Lee University**. Forty miles further north on I-81 is Staunton, a good place to end off the day.

THIRD DAY: A drive of just under one hour this morning brings you to the town of New Market, home of the **New Market Battle-field Park**, another Civil War place of interest. About 15 miles east on US 211 are the beautiful **Luray Caverns**. One of the most famous of America's caverns, the guided tours along well lighted path-ways will bring you past some amazing limestone formations. After Luray, take US 340 north 25 miles to the town of Front Royal, the northern gateway to Shenandoah National Park and your home for the night.

FOURTH DAY: Refer to the chapter on **Shenandoah National Park** to plan your activities here. At the park's southern terminus in the town of Waynesboro, Skyline Drive changes its name to the Blue Ridge Parkway. This national parkway continues along the crest of the Blue Ridge for a total of 470 miles, all the way to the **Great Smoky Mountains National Park**. As most of your day will have been spent in Shenandoah National Park, you will just cover a small section of the parkway today to reach the town of Buena Vista. On the way, be sure to stop at **Humpback Rocks Visitor Center** (Mile 5.8 from the beginning of the Parkway), and the **Peaks of Otter Visitor Center** (Mile 86).

FIFTH DAY: All day along the Blue Ridge Parkway with numerous stops on or just off it at **Rocky Knob** (Mile 169), **Mabry Mill** (Mile 176), **Grandfather Mountain** – an area of outstanding vistas and natural habitats for wildlife near Mile 306 – and the **Linville Falls Recreation Area** (Mile 316). You will also pass many scenic over-looks where you might want to linger a few moments. You should plan on spending the night at the town of Linville Falls after a day of majestic views and quaint towns.

SIXTH DAY: The **Craggy Gardens** at Mile 365 are at an elevation over 6,000 feet. Trails lead to beautiful vistas. The gardens them-selves are especially beautiful in mid-June when the rhododen-drons are in full bloom. You will exit the Blue Ridge Parkway just 25 miles later and enter the city of Asheville. The main attraction here is the **Biltmore House and Gardens**, where the magnificent gardens and the 255-room mansion are located on a tree-filled estate of over 7,500 acres. Ah, the rich knew how to live in days gone by! This was at one time the home of Cornelius Vanderbilt.

After Asheville you can reach the Smoky Mountains by getting back on the Blue Ridge Parkway, which loops south and then westward through some of the Southern Highlands' best scenery. However, an alternative is to head west by I-40 to US 19. This will take you to the Smoky's more quickly and along the way you can stop at **Maggie Valley's Ghost Town in the Sky**, a western theme park that the entire family is sure to enjoy. Further west at Cherokee is the southern end of the **Great Smoky Mountains National Park**, where you can spend the night.

SEVENTH DAY: The town of **Cherokee** has several interesting museums and visitor centers dedicated to the Cherokee Indians and they are worth a look before entering the park. **Great Smoky Mountains National Park** will take up the better part of the day. The northern end of the park is the town of **Gatlinburg**, Tennessee, where there are numerous attractions. Between the remainder of this afternoon and tomorrow morning you should see the **American Historical Wax Museum**; **Ober Gatlinburg**, reached by a breathtaking ride on the aerial tramway; and **Christus Gardens**, which depict scenes from the life of Christ in a beautiful setting (worthwhile whatever your religious persuasion).

EIGHTH DAY: Having completed the attractions in Gatlinburg by the middle of the day, you have just a hop, skip, and a jump to the town of Pigeon Forge and the **Dollywood Theme Park**. This attraction recreates a 19th-century Smoky Mountain community and also traces the career of Dolly Parton. Plan on spending several hours, which will still allow you to reach Knoxville by the end of the touring day.

NINTH DAY: For those ending their trip here, the morning will be available to see the city's sights, especially the **Confederate Memorial Hall**, **Governor William Blount Mansion** and the campus of the **University of Tennessee**, home of the Volunteers.

Extension to Mammoth Cave

Those of you who choose to add the 600 miles necessary to see Mammoth Cave National Park should leave Knoxville by mid-day and travel north on I-75 to the town of London, where you will then head west via SR 80 and the Cumberland Parkway. Spend the night in Cave City, just outside the park, or within the park itself.

TENTH DAY: The entire day will be devoted to the impressive **Mammoth Cave National Park**.

ELEVENTH DAY: To make the 600-mile trip to Mammoth Cave even more worthwhile, today you can head south along I-65, arriving before lunch time in Nashville. **Nashville** is a city with so much to do that it is not within the scope of this book even to list the possibilities. You could easily spend several days visiting **Opryland**, with its dozens of rides and fabulous shows (including one on an authentic show boat), the **Country Music Hall of Fame** and other attractions. You can spend the rest of this and the next two days here.

FOURTEENTH DAY: Traveling due east on I-40 you'll be back in Knoxville by around lunch time, where you can make connections to your home city.

Amid the Black Hills

PARK HIGHLIGHTS: Badlands National Monument (South Dakota); Devils Tower National Monument (Wyoming); Mount Rushmore National Memorial (South Dakota). Optional Extension to Scotts Bluff National Monument (Nebraska).

GATEWAY: Rapid City, South Dakota

ESTIMATED MILES: 610 (995 with extension)

TIME: 6 days (7 with extension)

FIRST DAY: Just north of the Rapid City airport, take I-90 east to the town of Wall, your overnight stopping place. Whether you arrive in late afternoon or evening, be sure to make time for visiting **Wall Drug**, which must certainly rank as one of the world's most unusual retailers.

SECOND DAY: Continue east on I-90 about 25 miles to the Cactus Flat exit and enter the **Badlands National Park**, allowing all morning for this attraction. Return on I-90, this time westbound, and take it for 1½ hours to the US 14A exit at Sturgis. From here it is a short ride to the towns of Deadwood and Lead. In the area, be sure to visit the still active **Homestake Gold Mine** and stroll the old and quaint, narrow streets of these towns which contain many attractions for visitors – especially the gift shops.

THIRD DAY: Continue on US 14A through the scenic northern portion of the **Black Hills National Forest** until it reaches I-90 at

Spearfish, and then on I-90 west to US 14 at Sundance, which will take you to the next major destination of your trip, **Devils Tower National Monument**. The ride should take just over two hours.

By afternoon you will have completed Devils Tower and will be making your way south via SR 585 and US 85. Stop at Newcastle to visit the **Accidental Oil Company**, a short break in your return to the Black Hills which will give you an idea of what oil prospecting was like in the old days. Then, just 24 miles further on US 16 is **Jewel Cave National Monument**, where a guided tour of caverns considered by some to be among the most beautiful in the country, awaits you. After that, a short ride up the road is Custer – a convenient town to make your base in the Black Hills.

FOURTH DAY: Today is the day for seeing what the beautiful Black Hills have to offer. A detailed map of the area is essential to avoid a lot of driving around in circles. Begin your tour with **Custer State Park**. One of the major highlights of this vast park will be the **Wildlife Loop Road**, where a herd of bison can be seen in their natural habitat. Do not get out of your car! Not only is it dangerous but it's unnecessary because these large animals will frequently be almost on top of your car. After the Loop Road work your way north on SR 87, which will take you through a section of the park called the **Needles Highway**. The eroded rock formations in this area are as incredible as any you will see in a national park, especially one called **The Eye of the Needle**. A few miles north of this area is the town of Hill City, where you can take a ride on the **1880 Train** through a remote portion of the Black Hills for some more great scenery.

Then work your way around on US 16 and SR 244 into **Mount Rushmore National Memorial**. You should arrive here late in the afternoon, so you can finish the daylight activities, then have dinner at the memorial and stay for the evening program before returning to Custer.

FIFTH DAY: The main attraction in town that you should not miss is the **Chief Crazy Horse Monument** which, when completed, will be larger than Mount Rushmore. The area includes an observation deck (where you might see blasting of the monument taking place), shops and museums. The **Western Woodcarvings** are also worth the time to visit before leaving town. Then head north on US 16A, again across Custer State Park, and begin your adventure on **Iron Mountain Road**, a fascinating engineering accomplishment with spiraling turns (the road is actually quite easy as long as you aren't driving a trailer) and beautiful scenery. An especially noteworthy stop is the **Norbeck Overlook**, where a distant view of Mount Rushmore will keep you riveted to the spot.

Now head for Rapid City on US 16, a scenic route properly known as Mount Rushmore Road. There are several attractions you might find interesting (especially if you have children in your group), including the **Reptile Gardens, Bear Country USA** and the **Rockerville Ghost Town**. You will arrive at Rapid City in the early evening.

SIXTH DAY: See the **Chapel in the Hills** just west of town on SR 44 and the **Geology Museum** at the South Dakota School of Mines in town before returning to the airport for your journey home.

Extension to Scotts Bluff

The trip will be the same until you have finished Newcastle on the Third Day. If you are taking this extension, continue south on US 85 for a long and, unfortunately, rather dull drive to the town of Torrington. Before checking in, take a short detour west on US 26 to **Fort Laramie National Historic Site**, a reconstructed frontier army post.

FOURTH DAY: From Torrington it is about an hour via US 26 eastbound to **Scotts Bluff National Monument**. Although it is not particularly large in area compared to most others in this book, you can spend a good deal of time at this unusual and beautiful formation. In the afternoon head to your overnight destination in Hot Springs via SR 71, US 20 and US 385.

FIFTH DAY: Head north into **Custer State Park** and pick up the itinerary from the fourth day of the trip without the extension.

SIXTH AND SEVENTH DAYS: The same as the fifth and sixth days without the extension.

Colorado Circle

PARK HIGHLIGHTS: Black Canyon of the Gunnison National Monument; Colorado National Monument; Mesa Verde National Park; Rocky Mountain National Park (all Colorado).

GATEWAY: Denver, Colorado

ESTIMATED MILES: 1,410

TIME: 13 days

FIRST DAY: There is lots to do in Denver – including plenty of cultural attractions – before you head into the beautiful country-side of Colorado. The **Denver Museum of Natural History** in City Park and the **Denver Art Museum** in Civic Center are the most noteworthy. But you should take time to see the gold-topped **State Capitol**, the **United States Mint** and the historic **Brown Palace Hotel**, all within a few blocks of one another in the compact downtown area. Good views of the distant Rockies are available from either City or Cheesman Parks.

SECOND DAY: On the western fringe of the city and surrounding suburbs is the **Red Rocks Park Amphitheater**, where shows are performed on summer evenings. By day, the natural amphitheater is a beautiful sight. Also, **Lookout Mountain** in the suburb of Golden offers breathtaking views along with the grave site of William (Buffalo Bill) Cody and a museum about the man and his legend. If the weather is clear, the view of Denver is spectacular. Turn around and the view is of the Rockies. Afterwards, make your way back towards the city on SR 58 to SR 121 (Wadsworth Blvd). This will take you to US 36 and directly into Boulder, a drive of under an hour. This attractive community in the foothills of the Rockies contains the beautiful tile-roofed campus of the **University of Colorado** and the **National Center for Atmospheric Research**, where self-guided tours are available.

You will now head for the Rockies using the most scenic route: SR 119 to SR 72 and finally SR 7 to the town of **Estes Park**, where you can spend the night. The scenery along the way is splendid, especially the view of Twin Sisters Peaks. The town of Estes Park is an exceptionally attractive mountain resort and is loaded with visitor facilities.

THIRD DAY: All morning and part of the afternoon today should be devoted to **Rocky Mountain National Park**. You will leave the park at Granby and head down US 40 east through Winter Park and the Berthoud Pass. The road is well-maintained, but there are some very sharp grades and hairpin turns. Magnificent alpine scenery surrounds you on all sides. Use low gear and always be alert for trucks, as this is a major through-road. The town of **Georgetown**, just off of I-70, exemplifies the grand mining era of Colorado history; it will also be your home for this evening. There are many interesting sights in town and pamphlets describing walking tours of the historic area are widely available in town.

FOURTH DAY: I-70 west through the Rockies is one of the most scenic interstate highways in the country. The **Eisenhower Tunnel** is among the greatest of engineering achievements. Stop for a brief rest at the beautiful **Keystone Resort** in Dillon; the views are fantastic here. But allow for a much longer hiatus in **Vail** which, if it weren't for the signs in English, could easily be mistaken for a Swiss Alpine village and ski resort. A shopper's paradise, Vail has the atmosphere of an outdoor mall. Leave I-70 for now at the US 24 exit and go to **Leadville**, where there are interesting historic attractions relating to the town's mining era. At an elevation of over 10,000 feet, it is one of the highest communities in the nation. Fifteen miles after Leadville, head north on SR 82, stopping at **Aspen** overnight. Be sure to take the short bus ride to the **Maroon Bells** (no private cars allowed), which are reputedly the most photographed mountains in all of Colorado.

FIFTH DAY: SR 82 will take you back to I-70. By lunch time you will be in the town of Grand Junction. After filling up your tank, continue past the town to the Fruita exit and head into the **Colo-**

rado National Monument. The unbelievable sights created here by erosion will more than satisfy you for the remainder of the afternoon. From here it is not far to your overnight accommodations in the town of Montrose – about 45 minutes from the eastern end of the monument via US 50.

SIXTH DAY: Thirty-six miles south of Montrose on US 550 is the town of Ouray, where you should see 20-foot-wide Box Canyon and the Bachelor-Syracuse Mine. A mine tram at the latter will take you a half-mile into Gold Hill. South from Ouray, US 550 is called the Million Dollar Highway. The trip is worth that price as it must certainly rank with the most impressive auto routes anywhere. For now, bypass the town of Silverton and continue on the scenic US 550 through the San Juan Mountains on into the town of Durango. Take the road slowly, not only because of the many turns, but so that you can admire the beauty around you. In Durango there are numerous historic attractions, including the Victorian-era Strater Hotel. There is a fun-filled chuck wagon dinner show available at the Bar-X, if western food and entertainment catch your fancy.

SEVENTH DAY: Allow all day for your ride on the narrow gauge Silverton Railroad. You'll really be able to appreciate the scenery as the train winds its way through narrow canyons, because you won't have to be on the lookout as a driver. Opportunities for pictures abound. Time is allowed in the town of Silverton for lunch and to explore the many quaint shops. Be sure to make reservations for the train trip, preferably several months in advance; this is a very popular excursion.

EIGHTH DAY: About an hour west of Durango on US 160 is the entrance to Mesa Verde National Park. After you have completed your visit to the park, head north on SR 145 (10 miles further west from the park exit). This scenic route will take you to your overnight accommodations in the town of Telluride, another of Colorado's numerous colorful historic mining communities.

NINTH DAY: Departing this morning via SR 145, SR 62 and US 550 back to Montrose, you will then travel on US 50 east. After a total ride (from Telluride) of about two hours, you will reach the Black Canyon of the Gunnison National Monument. You may think you have enough, but this will really open your eyes! Just east of the national monument is the Curecanti National Recreation Area. The road through it is beautiful; there are several dams and visitor centers scattered along the way, which makes this much more than just another scenic road. Afterwards, continue east on US 50 until you reach the town of Canon City. You'll spend the night here.

TENTH DAY: Among the amazing sights created by the Arkansas River just west of Canon City is the 1,200-foot-deep **Royal Gorge**. There is an aerial tramway and suspension bridge across the gorge and an incline railway that descends to the bottom of the canyon. There is also a miniature railroad with a pleasant ride and some fine views. For the more daring, the three-mile **Skyline Drive** provides additional vistas along a somewhat difficult one-way route. Ten minutes past Canon City you will head north on SR 115 and, 36 miles later, arrive in Colorado Springs, a city with an unusually high number of worthwhile attractions.

During the rest of this day and the eleventh day, you should plan on seeing the following attractions: **The Cave of the Winds, Garden of the Gods** (a "park" with over 900 acres of unusual red sandstone formations), **North Cheyenne Canyon** and the **Seven Falls**, as well as the famous **Pike's Peak Cog Railway**. You can also climb Pike's Peak by car, but make sure that your car is in top-notch condition. The drive is difficult.

In Colorado Springs itself, time permitting, you might also consider visiting the beautiful **Broadmore Hotel**, the **United States Olympic Complex** and the **Prorodeo Hall of Champions**.

TWELFTH DAY: Just a few miles north of Colorado Springs is the majestic **United States Air Force Academy**. The buildings are strikingly modern and the setting in the foothills of the Rockies is superb. Be sure to enter the famous Cadet Chapel, which is especially beautiful on a sunny day (which you will most likely have here during the summer); the stained glass captures the sunlight in a dazzling array of colors.

Afterwards it is only about a one-hour drive back to Denver. Use the rest of the afternoon to catch some more of the city sights, especially the historic **Larimer Square** and the **Elitch Gardens**, which combines an amusement park with floral displays reminiscent of Denmark's Tivoli. Seeing Denver's remaining attractions will take you into the morning of the thirteenth day and your return home.

Trip 4

Southwest Sojourn

PARK HIGHLIGHTS: Big Bend National Park (Texas); Carlsbad, Caverns National Park (New Mexico)

GATEWAY: El Paso, Texas

ESTIMATED MILES: 1,025

TIME: 6 days

FIRST DAY: This afternoon you should have time to capture at least some of the flavor of Mexico by visiting Ciudad Juarez on the opposite side of the Rio Grande. Border crossing for a same-day visit is a snap. See the **Mission of Our Lady of Guadalupe** and the ultra-modern **PRONAF Center**, but don't forget to visit some of the local markets. Back in El Paso for the night, catch the evening performance of *Viva! El Paso!*, which documents area history.

SECOND DAY: The major scenic sight of El Paso is the **aerial tramway** ride to Ranger Peak in the northern part of the city. Views from here extend back into Mexico. Excellent vistas are also available from **Scenic Drive**, which passes through the rugged Franklin Mountains. Other interesting attractions include the **Bullfight Museum, Chazimal National Monument**, which commemorates the peaceful U.S.-Mexican border, and the **Fort Bliss Replica Museum**. Then head out of town following I-10 east along the Rio Grande Valley to your overnight stop at Van Horn.

THIRD DAY: About 37 miles past Van Horn, exit from the interstate onto SR 118. In about half an hour you will reach SR 166, a scenic loop into Fort Davis. In town itself is the **Fort Davis National Historic Site.** Then go north on SR 118 to the **W. J. McDonald Observatory,** which contains one of the world's largest telescopes. Reverse your route through Fort Davis and continue on SR 118 all the way to **Big Bend National Park,** where overnight accommodations are available.

FOURTH DAY: You will be kept occupied at Big Bend until well into the afternoon. Upon leaving the park via SR 385, continue for approximately 100 miles to the town of **Fort Stockton.** Before calling it a day, stretch your legs with a walking tour of the historic downtown (brochures are available from the Chamber of Commerce).

FIFTH DAY: From Fort Stockton it is a three-hour drive north via US 285 and US 62/80 to **Carlsbad Caverns National Park.** Overnight accommodations can be found in nearby communities. The chapter on Carlsbad Caverns outlines sightseeing activities for the entire afternoon and evening.

SIXTH DAY: Heading west on US 62/180, you will soon arrive back in Texas at the **Guadalupe Mountains National Park.** Although not a well-developed park as yet, there are some nice vistas, including 8,749-foot Guadalupe Peak, highest point in the Lone Star State. Some 90 miles past the park is a short cutoff road (FM 2775) which will take you to the **Hueco Tanks State Park,** site of some unusual geologic formations. From here you will be able to make it back to El Paso by early afternoon.

Trip 5

Scenery Unlimited

PARK HIGHLIGHTS: Craters Of The Moon National Monument (Idaho); Glacier National Park (Montana); Grand Teton National Park (Wyoming); Yellowstone National Park (Wyoming).

GATEWAY: Great Falls, Montana

ESTIMATED MILES: 1,525 (1,685 with side trip)

TIME: 10 days (11 with side trip)

FIRST DAY: You begin your trip to these four outstanding natural attractions and much more by seeing the **C. M. Russell Museum** in town, devoted to the works of the great western artist. **The Falls** and the adjacent **Big Springs** make a worthwhile visit and are located just east of the city.

SECOND DAY: Heading south on scenic I-15 it is about an hour ride to the **Gates of the Mountains Wilderness**. A boat ride will take you between immense, towering cliffs on a journey up the Missouri River. Allow two hours for the round-trip cruise and walking through the area. Then it is a short ride into Helena, where the **State Capitol** awaits, along with the magnificent **Cathedral of Helena**. Also plan on taking the **Last Chancer**, a narrated tram or bus tour of the city's colorful past. Continue south on I-15 through a particularly scenic section that crosses the Continental Divide and arrive a bit later in Butte, your overnight stop for this evening. Be sure to look into the open pit **Berkeley Mine**.

THIRD DAY: About 30 miles east of Butte off I-90 is the **Lewis and Clark Caverns State Park**. Two-hour tours through the cavern will likely leave you agreeing that it is one of the most beautiful in the country, even though not well known. Be advised that the tours are strenuous. Then get back on I-90 for an hour or so. Exit onto US 89 at Livingston for the dramatic approach to the northern entrance of **Yellowstone National Park**. The remainder of today and all of your fourth day will be in Yellowstone, as will the morning of the fifth day. Two nights accommodation in the park should be arranged far in advance.

FIFTH DAY: Leaving Yellowstone in mid-morning, it is a short drive via the beautiful John D. Rockefeller Memorial Highway into **Grand Teton National Park**. Spend the remainder of the day amid the splendid alpine scenery. Overnight is in **Jackson**, just below the south entrance of the park. Be sure to see the stage robbery and gunfight in the town square, held every evening in summer. You can also pass the evening by browsing the shops of this town where the sidewalks are old-fashioned western boardwalks.

SIXTH DAY: Head west from town on SR 22 and into Idaho (SR 33 and 31 to US 26 westbound). Arriving by mid-morning at **Idaho Falls**, stop to see the picturesque cataract that gives the town its name. It is best viewed from an attractive park along the Snake River. Continue west along US 20. In about two hours you will arrive at **Craters of the Moon National Monument**, the third of the four park highlights of this journey. After leaving the monument, continue on US 20 until SR 75. Arrival in Ketchum will be late.

SEVENTH DAY: Take a while to explore the beautiful **Sun Valley** ski resorts this morning before continuing the northern trek. You will be traveling through the beautiful **Sawtooth National Recreation Area** where you should stop at the visitor center and admire the scenery. Leaving the recreation area, SR 75 links up with US 93 northbound and is called the Salmon River Scenic Route. You'll find it is appropriately named. While you may not tire of the scenery, you probably will become a bit mileage weary, so plan on spending the night at Hamilton, Montana. Do see the **Daly Mansion**, the former estate of a copper baron.

EIGHTH DAY: Your route continues on US 93. The scenery becomes grander as you come to **Flathead Lake**, with views not only of the lake but of the valley and surroundinig mountains as well. A boat ride on the lake is a good way to see everything and to take a break from driving. Then get on US 2 eastbound at Kalispell. This road will bring you to **Glacier National Park**. But before you get there, make a short detour at **Hungry Horse** to see the dam and beautiful **Hungry Horse Reservoir**. There is a road around the reservoir, but it is mostly unpaved. Overnight can be at West Glacier, right at the entrance to the park, or at one of the hotels just inside the park (Apgar area).

NINTH DAY: You can spend all day in **Glacier National Park**. See Chapter 14 for details. Upon exiting the east end of the park at St. Mary, the trip can go one of two ways. The short way is to head south on US 89 and SR 49 to East Glacier Park. There are overnight accommodations and a few more attractions in the park from another entrance here.

Option: A better idea upon leaving St. Mary is to head north on US 93 and re-enter the park at Babb. Stay overnight at Many Glacier. The next day take the Chief Joseph Highway into Canada and visit **Waterton Lakes National Park**; a special section at the end of Chapter 14 has details on this area. Then retrace your route south, continuing on US 93 to East Glacier as above. This detour adds 160 miles and exactly one day to the trip. I highly recommend it: both Many Glacier and Waterton Lakes are breathtaking. Continue with the tenth day of the basic trip, which will actually be your eleventh if you do this option.

TENTH DAY: In about three hours, US 2 and 89 will bring you back to Great Falls and your voyage home. The fantastic sights along the way will make you wish that the trip was going to continue; but, alas, all good things must end. Even so, with Yellowstone, Grand Teton and Glacier National Parks behind you, you will have seen three of the very best parks in the national park system.

Trip 6

Going to the Canyons

PARK HIGHLIGHTS: Grand Canyon National Park; Glen Canyon National Recreation Area; Petrified Forest National Park (all Arizona); Rainbow Bridge National Monument (Utah).

GATEWAY: Phoenix, Arizona

ESTIMATED MILES: 990 (1,210 including Grand Canyon North Rim)

TIME: 7 days (8 including Grand Canyon North Rim)

FIRST DAY: Your first afternoon should focus on the **Desert Botanical Garden**. This is part of Papago Park in the eastern corner of the city, just before the Scottsdale border. Desert plants of the world are displayed on over 150 acres. The best time to visit is in the blooming season from late March through May. If time allows, then you can also visit the **Arizona State Capitol** and the **Old State Capitol**, which is now a museum devoted to the history of the state.

SECOND DAY: Heading north on I-17, about 80 miles north of the city limits you will arrive at **Montezuma Castle National Monument**. This is a fine example of prehistoric cliff dwellings, dating from the 12th century. It is remarkably well preserved. To keep it that way, the five-story, 20-room structure is closed to visitors. But the exterior view is worth the trip and the visitor center provides interesting background information.

Just north of Montezuma Castle you will exit the interstate highway onto SR 179, which runs into US 89A at the town of Sedonia near the entrance to **Oak Creek Canyon**. The narrow canyon is 16 miles long and has been made famous by the many Western movies made here. The movie makers were attracted by the unusually sunny weather, the magnificent multi-colored rocks, and the lush vegetation. The road is narrow and twisting but it is not terribly difficult to drive. You emerge from the canyon at Flagstaff, where you will be able to pick up US 180 and take an easy 80-mile drive over surprisingly level terrain to the **Grand Canyon National Park**. Your arrival at the South Rim comes up quite unexpectedly, with no hint of what awaits until you are almost there. The night can be spent on the South Rim. There will be little time for sightseeing on this day, but do try to get a glimpse of the Canyon at sunset!

THIRD DAY: You can spend most of the day seeing the South Rim. Departing the park in the late afternoon, you will be passing through an area (SR 64) known as the **Little Colorado River Gorge**. Although not as spectacular as the Grand Canyon, the twisting roadway takes you through some beautiful country. Turning north on US 89 at Cameron, you will have to travel 75 miles before reaching your next destination at Marble Canyon. This is a part of the **Glen Canyon National Recreation Area**, where you will spend the evening.

Note: An optional trip to the **North Rim of the Grand Canyon** can be made the next day. It will add exactly one day to the trip: you can get to the North Rim, see the sights and return to Marble Canyon by the end of the day. If you choose this option, remember that it will add 220 miles to the basic itinerary. Also, each day listed from here on is to be one day later (i.e., the fourth day becomes the fifth day, and so forth).

FOURTH DAY: From Marble Canyon it is about one hour via US 89A and 89 to the pleasant town of Page, where the bulk of your activities in the **Glen Canyon National Recreation Area** will take place. Consult Chapter 15 for details, including an excellent half-day boat trip to **Rainbow Bridge National Monument**.

FIFTH DAY: Retrace your route down US 89, this time going beyond Cameron until you arrive at the **Wupatki National Monument** and, 12 miles beyond that, **Sunset Crater National Monument**. The former is another impressive area of Indian ruins, while Sunset Crater is what is left of a volcanic cone. Just south of Sunset Canyon you again reach Flagstaff, where I-40 eastbound will take you on a pleasant drive through the **Painted Desert** region of Arizona. A stop should be made at **Meteor Crater**, just six miles off of the interstate. While not the most beautiful sight in the state, this gigantic hole is undoubtedly impressive. You inevitably ponder what might be the consequences if a meteor of such size were to hit the earth today. A bit further on you can stop for the evening at the town of Holbrook.

SIXTH DAY: About 25 miles east of Holbrook on the interstate you will come to the northern entrance of the **Petrified Forest National Park**. You should allow a few hours to tour the park then, from its southern end, go west on US 180 back to Holbrook. There you can pick up SR 77 and take it to the junction of US 60 in Show-Low. Head west on scenic US 60 to your evening's destination, Globe. The canyon of the Salt River that you traversed on your way to Globe contains several small state parks with excellent views.

SEVENTH DAY: On leaving Globe you have a choice. The easy way back to Phoenix is to continue all the way with US 60, which will get you back to the city in just under two hours, leaving some time to explore sights in Phoenix such as **South Mountain Park**. Or, if you prefer, you can return via the Apache Trail (SR 88). This option adds 30 miles to your route, with some parts of the narrow, twisting road paved only in gravel. This route will reward you with an ever-changing series of vistas, including the **Superstition Mountains, Fish Creek Canyon** and several picturesque mountain lakes. If you take this route there will be no time for sightseeing in Phoenix unless you tack on another day.

Trip 7

Color Country

PARK HIGHLIGHTS: Arches National Park; Bryce Canyon National Park; Canyonlands National Park; Capitol Reef National Park (all Utah); Lake Mead National Recreation Area (Nevada/Arizona); Zion National Park (Utah).

GATEWAY: Las Vegas

ESTIMATED MILES: 1,670

TIME: 10 days (longer if you want more time in Las Vegas)

FIRST DAY: I have always found that Las Vegas is a great place to end a trip, especially a long one like this. So resist the temptation to linger when you first arrive in town. Get in the car and head out on I-15 northbound. The drive through the desert is not particularly exciting, except briefly when the road cuts across the extreme northwest corner of Arizona and weaves its way through colorful mountains. Altogether, it will be 3½ hours to your overnight stop at Cedar City.

SECOND DAY: You will find that nowhere on earth is the scenery quite like the Color Country of southern Utah. And we'll get our first glimpse this morning – **Cedar Breaks National Monument** is only a short distance from Cedar City off of SR 14. Its pink cliffs will give you a foretaste of things to come. Unfortunately, because of the limited road network in southern Utah, a result of difficult terrain and the sparse population, there will be more than the usual amount of driving overlap and the distances involved will sometimes be great. On the bright side, we will get through a big chunk of this mileage today while you are comparatively fresh, allowing more time for sightseeing in the days to come.

From Cedar Breaks, SR 143 leads back into I-15, which you take north two exits to SR 20. Then pick up US 89 north to SR 62. This road ends at SR 24, on which you will be driving east, passing through Capitol Reef National Park (do not stop now!), then arriving in Hanksville for the evening.

THIRD DAY: Head south this morning on SR 95 for about 100 miles through more scenery to **Natural Bridges National Monument**. Three bridges in various stages of geologic evolution are visible from the eight-mile loop road or by short, easy walks. Continue on SR 95 until you reach US 191. This road, heading north, will take you to Moab, your overnight lodging place. Before reaching town, however, be sure to take the side road to the Needles Section of **Canyonlands National Park**; also stop to see **Wilson Arch** (23 miles south of Moab, right alongside the road) and **Hole-'n-the Rock**. The latter, just south of town, is a home that has actually been excavated out of a large sandstone rock formation.

FOURTH DAY: Your visit to the main section of **Canyonlands National Park** will take up most of the morning. Afterwards, stop at nearby **Dead Horse State Park** for an unforgettable and dramatic view of the Colorado River far below. This afternoon will be devoted entirely to **Arches National Park**. All these attractions are close to one another so you won't have to spend much time getting from one to the other. If you are visiting in summer you might want to do Arches in the morning and Canyonlands in the afternoon because you will be doing more walking in Arches – and that is best done in the morning when it is cooler. Return to Moab for the evening and take a pleasant boat ride ("Canyonlands By Night") on the Colorado River. The majestic formations are floodlit and there is interesting commentary, creating an experience quite different from your daytime touring.

FIFTH DAY: Drive north on US 191 to I-70, then west to SR 24 westbound. The 51 miles from Hanksville to Torrey is a repeat drive, but this time you will be stopping for a detailed look at **Capitol Reef National Park**. Overnight at the nearby town of Bicknell.

SIXTH DAY: Today you will be travelling via SR 12, the highly scenic Boulder-Escalante Highway. Stop at **Kodachrome Basin**

State Park. As you can tell from the name, this park features very colorful formations. But they are no match for what comes 15 miles further: **Bryce Canyon National Park**. Arriving in late morning, you should be on the rim of this truly unforgettable canyon until near sundown, as that will allow you to see it in all different shades of light. You'll be spending the evening either just north of the park entrance or inside the park itself. Either way you might want to check in and relax for a while on your way in.

SEVENTH DAY: It is just a couple of hours from Bryce to **Zion National Park** and the ride is a pleasant and colorful one. Leaving Bryce, SR 12 passes through **Red Canyon** (which gives you a hint of what you will see up ahead). Turn south on US 89 until you reach SR 9 westbound. This is the famous **Zion-Mount Carmel Highway**, an outstanding achievement in mountain road building. The terrain is rough but the ride is surprisingly easy. The end of this portion of SR 9 brings you into magnificent Zion National Park. After spending practically the entire day here, you can continue on SR 9 to I-15 and your evening accommodations in the town of St. George.

EIGHTH DAY: Now you will double back on I-15 until well into Nevada at the Overton turnoff and the entrance to **Lake Mead National Recreation Area**. Before going too far into the recreation area, however, you should take a short detour west at the road junction for Overton Beach and see the **Valley of Fire State Park** with its impressive formations and prehistoric petroglyphs. Then proceed with your day-long journey through the many sights and activities in the Lake Mead National Recreation Area. Leaving the recreation area at Boulder City, Las Vegas is only an hour away via US 93. Although you'll probably arrive in early evening you still have time to take in a show or do some gaming if you desire.

NINTH DAY: How long you spend in Las Vegas will depend on how much you like to gamble or relax by the pool and how many shows you want to take in. But you should plan on spending at least two nights and probably an additional two to three if this is your first visit. In addition to gaming activities and shows, a major tourist pastime is visiting all the large, lavish hotels. Don't miss downtown's **Fremont Street Casino Center** at night. It makes Broadway's "Great White Way" seem dull by comparison. Other attractions in Las Vegas are the **Liberace Museum**, the **Palace Auto Collection**, tours of the behind-the-scenes activities at the **Mint Casino**, **Omnimax Theater at Caesar's Palace**, the volcano in front of the **Mirage Hotel** ("erupts" after dark), and the midway and performances at the **Circus Circus Hotel**.

Trip 8

The Cascades & Olympic Odyssey

PARK HIGHLIGHTS: Mount Rainier National Park; North Cascades National Park/Ross Lake National Recreation Area; Olympic National Park (all Washington).

GATEWAY: Seattle, Washington

ESTIMATED MILES: 960

TIME: 8 days

FIRST AND SECOND DAYS: When you visit Seattle you will understand why it is consistently listed among the best places to live in the United States. The Emerald City is really a gem. During the two days allocated to see its sights, don't miss the **Seattle Center**, former site of the World's Fair and now containing the Pacific Science Center and the Space Needle. At nearly 600 feet, the needle gives you a view of not only the impressive downtown skyline, but Lake Washington and Puget Sound (between which Seattle is snugly nestled) as well as the mountains. If you are lucky enough to have a very clear day you will see Mount Rainier "floating" above the city. Downtown are the **Klondike Gold Rush National Historic Park** (Pioneer Square), the fun-filled **Pike Place Market** and the **waterfront**, which can be explored on foot or by trolley. The Pike Street Hillclimb connects the two. Museum enthusiasts can choose among the **Seattle Art Museum** and those devoted to area history and culture, such as the **Burke Memorial**

Washington Museum or the **Museum of History and Industry**. Sports nuts might want to tour the **Kingdome**. A definite highlight is the **Lake Washington Ship Canal/Hiram Chittendam Locks** area. Not only will you see many colorful boats passing through the locks but there are attractive gardens and, most importantly, special viewing windows beneath the water's surface that allow you to watch salmon climbing the fish ladders.

THIRD DAY: Less than an hour north of Seattle via I-5 is Everett, where you can tour the mammoth **Boeing aircraft assembly facility**. Then continue north on I-5 to SR 20 at Burlington and head east into the mountains. Soon after, the road – North Cascades Highway – will become very scenic as you approach **North Cascades National Park** and **Ross Lake National Recreation Area**. Chapter 28 discusses both of these and a related attraction, the **Skagit Seattle City Light Tour**. Overnight should be spent in Diablo.

FOURTH DAY: Leaving this area in mid-morning, reverse your route and take SR 20 all the way west to **Whidby Island**. Good views of Puget Sound and the San Juan Islands can be had on this drive. At Keystone, a ferry will carry you and your car across to Port Townsend on the Olympic Peninsula. The Victorian town's **Fort Worden State Park** is worthwhile. Just beyond Port Townsend you will approach US 101. The next stop is Sequim, where the **Dungeness Spit State Park** and **Olympic Game Farm** are noted attractions. The spit extends over six miles into the Strait of Juan de Fuca. Overnight will be in Port Angeles.

FIFTH DAY: Olympic National Park is huge; it will take the entire day to see it. After circling the peninsula, you finish the day with overnight lodging in Aberdeen.

SIXTH DAY: US 12 and SR 8 east will bring you to the state capital of Olympia, where visiting the impressive **Capitol campus** will finish a pleasant morning. Then take I-5 north to SR 512 onto SR 7. At Elber, pick up SR 706 right into **Mount Rainier National Park**, arriving in late afternoon. Your overnight accommodations will be at the park headquarters site of Paradise and reservations should be made well in advance. (Consult Chapter 25 on what to see in the park between your point of entry and Paradise).

SEVENTH DAY: Touring the major part of Mount Rainier National Park will occupy most of the day. From the north entrance on SR 410, routes 164 and I-5 will return you before dinner time to Seattle, a two-hour trip.

EIGHTH DAY: You should have some time before your flight home to see attractions you didn't see earlier and be able to board the plane with outstanding memories of the Pacific Northwest's great beauty.

Trail of the Volcanoes

PARK HIGHLIGHTS: Crater Lake National Park (Oregon); Lassen Volcanic National Park (California); Mount St. Helens National Volcanic Monument (Oregon).

GATEWAY: Portland, Oregon

ESTIMATED MILES: 1,675

TIME: 9 days

FIRST DAY: An afternoon in Portland will give you time to explore the attractive downtown area as well as at least one example of its fine scenic parks – of which **Washington Park**, with its famous Rose and Japanese Gardens, is the best.

SECOND DAY: On the agenda for today is **Mount St. Helens National Volcanic Monument**. It can be visited from the east or west side, but the two are not closely linked by the mountain road system. So this itinerary will cover only the west side, which is more easily accessible. Head north from Portland on I-5 to Castle Rock exit (SR 504). It is just over 30 miles by this scenic route to the focus of visitor activities, but there are related attractions en route, as described in Chapter 27.

Now reverse your route. Take I-5 south to I-205 to I-84. This superhighway parallels the Columbia River Gorge, an area of remarkable beauty. Among your stops on I-84 (or just off it on the parallel "Old Highway") are **Crown Point**, which provides the best panorama of the gorge; famous **Multnomah Falls** (highest of the 11 falls along the Columbia River Highway); and the **Cascade Locks**. At the latter, where you will be spending the evening, are the extensive visitor facilities of the huge **Bonneville Dam** complex. Be sure to visit both the Oregon and Washington sides, which are connected by a bridge at this point. Beautiful grounds supplement interesting exhibits about the dam project.

THIRD DAY: A short distance further west on I-84 is Hood River. Take SR 35 south from here, stopping at **Panorama Point** for an excellent view of snow-covered **Mount Hood**. Continue on to the junction of US 26 and take this road east to Madras. Between here and the town of Bend there are numerous activities encompassing some spectacular scenery. In the Madras area is the **Cove Palisades State Park**, where three canyons carved by a river are set in the midst of a beautiful dammed lake. In Bend, south of Madras on US 97, are the **Oregon High Desert Museum** and **Pilot Butte State Park**, a 511-foot cinder cone with great views of the Cascade Range.

From Bend, the Cascade Lakes Highway winds through lakes, reservoirs, and past mountains, all amid the deep green cover of the **Deschutes National Forest**. Follow the Cascade Lakes Highway for 58 miles from Bend and then turn east at the junction leading back to US 97 at LaPine, where overnight accommodations are available.

FOURTH DAY: Leaving LaPine, follow US 97 south for 44 miles and then go west on SR 138 for 15 miles, which will bring you to the northern entrance of **Crater Lake National Park** (see Chapter 10). What has to be one of the world's most breathtaking sights, the blue hues of Crater Lake, will keep you spellbound for the entire day. From the park's south entrance, SR 62 runs back into US 97 and in under an hour you'll be at tonight's stopping point, Klamath Falls.

FIFTH DAY: From Klamath Falls, crossing into California, it is about 75 miles to I-5. Near the town of Weed there is a turnout on the road with a sweeping view of perpetually ice-clad **Mount Shasta**. You will be on I-5 southbound for only a short time, exiting at SR 89 and following this road to **McArthur Burney Falls Memorial State Park**. The 129-foot high falls are in a thickly forested area. Ahead, at the junction of SR 44, is **Subway Cave**. The quarter-mile-long lava tube is not for everyone; in some places the height of the tube is only four feet and there is a lot of bending required. Also, you must provide your own light, so bring along a good flashlight or lantern. From here SR 44 will, in less than half an hour, bring you to **Lassen Volcanic National Park**, where you can spend the entire afternoon, as described in Chapter 22. Leaving Lassen, it is 50 miles west on SR 36 to the town of Red Bluff and your overnight accommodations.

SIXTH DAY: Drive north on I-5 this morning for 50 miles to the **Whiskeytown-Shasta-Trinity National Recreation Area.** I-5 through this part of the recreation area provides some very pleasant scenery. In addition, at **Lake Shasta Caverns** there are guided tours of the cave located way up on the mountainside. You are transported to the cave entrance via boat and a short bus ride up the mountain.

Proceeding north once again on I-5, the remainder of the day will be spent in travel until you reach the night's destination in Roseburg, Oregon.

SEVENTH DAY: The **Wildlife Safari**, southwest of town on SR 42 is a drive-through park with more than 600 animals. There are also animal shows and other attractions. Continue on SR 42 and in less than two hours you reach the junction of US 101. From here north begins your tour of the Oregon coast, which most consider more spectacular than the Big Sur coast of California. First on the agenda is the picturesque lighthouse at **Umpqua Lighthouse State Park** and the **Oregon Dunes National Recreation Area.** There are several good places here to view the high sand dunes that drop precipitously to the sea. Half-hour sand dune buggy rides are available at Sand Dunes Frontier, four miles south of Florence. Plan to spend the night in Florence.

EIGHTH DAY: All day will be devoted to travelling the beautiful coast highway, which is an easy drive. Your first stop this morning is the **Sea Lion Caves.** An elevator takes you down to a cavern that measures over a quarter-mile long. Inside the caverns and outside on the sea coast's rocky bluffs there are many opportunities to watch the playful sea lions in their natural habitat.

Most of what you will see during the rest of the day will be vistas of the sea and unusual rock formations of all types. From south to north, you should be on the lookout for **Devils Elbow State Park** and **Cape Perpetua**, where a visitor center for the **Siuslaw National Forest** is perched high atop a rocky promontory. The cape is just off US 101 near the town of Yachats and it provides one of the best views along the entire coast. Continuing, see **Devil's Punch-**

bowl State Park, Otter Crest Wayside, Depot and **Boiler Bays** and the **D River Wayside** (the world's shortest river). A highly entertaining attraction in the town of Seal Rock is **Seal Gulch** – a quarter-mile trail "inhabited" by over 400 humorous sculptured wooden figures.

North of Lincoln City the coastal attractions are on a spur road off US 101 from Cloverdale to Tillamook: **Cape Lookout State Park, Cape Falcon** and **Ecola State Park** at Cannon Beach, the ending point for today's journey.

NINTH DAY: With memories of yesterday and the previous days still vivid, you can take US 26 back to Portland, a two-hour drive.

Trip 10

High Sierra Adventure

PARK HIGHLIGHTS: Sequoia and Kings Canyon National Parks; Yosemite National Park (all California).

GATEWAY: San Francisco, California

ESTIMATED MILES: 1,000

TIME: 10 days

FIRST THROUGH THIRD DAYS: Spend these days in San Francisco. The **Golden Gate, Fisherman's Wharf, Chinatown, cable cars, hilly Lombard Street, Nob Hill** and many other attractions have become symbolic of the City by the Bay.

FOURTH AND FIFTH DAYS: Leaving San Francisco, it is under four hours to the entrance of **Yosemite National Park** via I-580 east to I-205 and then SR 120. Filling up the afternoon and entire next day with seeing Yosemite should not be difficult. Your visit will probably concentrate on the famous valley and points south. To do the Tuolumne area in the park's northern region will add a day and about 150 additional miles. If you do so, each day below will be pushed back by one. See Chapter 36.

SIXTH DAY: Exiting the park on SR 41, it is just 95 miles from Yosemite Village to Fresno. The center of a productive agricultural region, this is a good place to visit one of the area's many wineries. Taking SR 180 west from Fresno you'll be at **Kings Canyon Na-**

tional Park by mid-afternoon, first visiting the Cedar Grove section of the park. Overnight accommodations are available in the park.

SEVENTH DAY: The major part of your tour through **Sequoia and Kings Canyon National Parks** (see Chapter 33) will be this morning using SR 198, which loops through sections of both parks.

Then continue on SR 198 to **Visalia**, where you can take a self-guided walking tour of the historic section of town, which dates from the mid-19th century. Leave SR 198 at SR 41 and head south until you reach SR 46. This road heads into Paso Robles and your overnight accommodations.

EIGHTH DAY: Head south this morning on US 101 to San Luis Obispo. Before picking up SR 1 to begin your journey north on the beautiful California coast, the **Mission San Luis Obispo** is well worth a visit.

And now for the dramatic coast. Fifteen miles north of San Luis Obispo is **Moro Bay**. Moro Rock is a cinder cone rising over 500 feet from the shallow bay, and it is easily seen from the road. Then, in under an hour you'll be at San Simeon, site of the **Hearst-San Simeon State Historic Monument**, more commonly known as Hearst Castle. This is one of the world's greatest mansions, and certainly one of the glitziest; it takes four separate tours, each lasting 1¾ hours, to see all of it. The tours do not duplicate one another except for the short, exciting bus ride from the roadside parking area up the narrow and winding mountain road to the main house. Unless you are really "into" houses, I suggest that you take no more than two or three tours so that you can finish your visit to San Simeon by day's end. In any event, reserve all tours in advance.

NINTH DAY: Although it is only 65 miles up SR 1 to your first stop of the day, allow two hours to drive the winding, scenic coast highway. **Pfeiffer Big Sur State Park**, commonly known simply as "Big Sur," is an outstanding area of seacoast and mountain scenery, along with huge redwood trees.

Another hour up the coast and you will arrive in the **Carmel-Monterey-Pacific Grove** area, your overnight stopping point and site of numerous attractions for this afternoon. Carmel is home to **Point Lobos State Reserve**, a rugged area of seacoast. Numerous sea lions make their home here. The **Seventeen Mile Drive** is in Pacific Grove and is a must-see on any trip here. Do get out for the short walk to one of America's most photographed spots – the **Lone Cypress Tree**. There are several other scenic spots along this private toll road, including some of the country's most famous golf courses. Monterey, although in a scenic setting, has attractions of a more historic nature: **Cannery Row** (now a chic shopping area), **Monterey State Historic Park** and **San Carlos Cathedral**. There is also a fine aquarium.

TENTH DAY: Do you know the way to San José? I hope so, because that is where you are headed this morning (Highway 101 gets you there). An attractive city, San José is home to the **Lick Observatory, Winchester Mystery House** (a spooky, fun-filled mansion) and a fine ancient **Egyptian Museum**.

If you want to extend your trip by another day, you can also visit Marriott's **Great America Amusement Park** in nearby Santa Clara. Otherwise, continue up US 101 and you will reach San Francisco airport by mid-afternoon.

Trip 11

Paradise Found

PARK HIGHLIGHTS: Haleakala National Park; Hawaii Volcanoes National Park (both Hawaii).

GATEWAY: Honolulu, Hawaii

ESTIMATED MILES: 675

TIME: At least 9 days

Because people differ as to how much time should be spent lying on the beach or taking in local entertainment and shopping (of which Hawaii has an abundance), it is really up to you how much time you allot for this trip. For this reason, we will depart from our usual day-by-day itinerary and, instead, highlight what should be seen on four of the main islands – Oahu, Kauai, Maui, and Hawaii. The order you see them in doesn't matter since inter-island flights are fast, frequent, and conveniently scheduled throughout the day. So, we'll deal with the islands in alphabetical order.

Hawaii

A loop drive around the entire island is both feasible and desirable. The main city, Hilo, has a number of scenic attractions, including **Akaka Falls State Park, Liliuokalani Gardens Park** and **Rainbow Falls**. Hilo is also the center of the islands' orchid growing industry and several of these colorful facilities are open to the public.

Nearby is the plantation and production center of Mauna Loa Macadamia Nuts.

A short drive south of Hilo is **Hawaii Volcanoes National Park**. As described in Chapter 20, you should allow the better part of a day to see it.

SRs 11 and 19 form a circle around the island. Major sights are the **Punaluu Black Sand Beach** in Pahula, the **Pu'uhonua o Honaunau** (City of Refuge) **National Historic Park**, the **Painted Church** in Keokea, and the **Parker Ranch** in Waimea. Hawaii's highest mountains – **Mauna Kea** (13,796 feet) and **Mauna Loa** (13,677 feet) – are visible from many points on the island. SR 200 leads near the top of Mauna Kea, but it is a rough drive.

Recreational facilities (and most hotels) on the Big Island are concentrated on the Kona Coast (Kailua) and, to a far lesser extent, in Hilo.

Kauai

The Garden Isle's airport at Lihue is near the resort area of Wailua. A number of major attractions are also in this vicinity, including boat rides to the famous **Fern Grotto** and a rock formation known as the **Sleeping Giant**. But the island's major scenic attraction is spectacular **Waimea Canyon**, a state reserve which compares with the best of the national parks in its beauty. SRs 50 and 500 lead there (round-trip from Wailua is about 100 miles). The 10-mile gorge has a number of viewpoints, the best being **Canyon Lookout** at an elevation of 3,400 feet. **Kokee State Park** is right after Waimea Canyon and has an overlook which allows you to see the rugged spectacular **Na Pali Coast**. The only way to fully appreciate this magnificent coastal area is by helicopter tour or boat trip, the latter leaving from the town of Hanalei on Kauai's north coast.

The Spouting Horn and **Olu Pua Gardens** can be visited on the way to Waimea Canyon to break up the ride. Spouting Horn is about five miles off of SR 50 via SR 520 or 530.

Maui

The Valley Isle is the most scenic of the major islands. Most of the major resorts are in the Kaanapali Beach area, but numerous others are scattered throughout the island.

A half-day is necessary to properly visit the second of this trip's park highlights – **Haleakala National Park** (see Chapter 19), accessible by winding SRs 378 and 37. But Maui has many other beautiful attractions. Among the most popular is the historic whaling town of **Lahaina** (near Kaanapali's resort area) and the **Iao Valley** in Wailuku. Within the valley is the famous Iao Needle, a vegetation-covered rock that rises about 1,300 feet above the floor of this tropical valley. **Maui Plantation** in Waikapu offers a guided tram tour of groves where some of the island's major crops are grown.

Two beautiful drives are also possible. One is SR 30 from Lahaina to Maakea. This 16-mile section of road presents dramatic views of sea and mountains. It is especially gorgeous at sunset. The other is the famous road to Hana (SR 360). The number of turns in the road has been counted at over 600, but there are also innumerable rewarding vistas, waterfalls and supposedly sacred Hawaiian pools for the adventurer who follows this road.

Oahu

Site of Honolulu, Oahu is the "Gathering Place." While the real Hawaii may be more readily found on the outer islands, Oahu does have many worthwhile attractions.

Honolulu offers the usual cultural amenities of any major city, but you will be more interested in the things that make it unique. Of course, touring the luxury hotels of Waikiki is popular (as is visiting the major resorts on the outer islands). The **Waikiki Beach** area is always humming with activity, especially at night. Spend some time strolling along **Kalakaua Avenue**, including the **International Market Place**. Be sure to visit the **National Cemetery of the Pacific**, known as the Punchbowl. Set in an extinct volcano crater, it not only is a beautiful and soul-stirring sight, but it provides one of the best views of Waikiki. Driving up to **Diamond Head**, adjacent to Waikiki, is another scenic attraction – the **Dole Pineapple Cannery** is also of interest. But perhaps the most important stop in

Honolulu is the *USS Arizona* **Memorial** at Pearl Harbor. This dramatic monument can be visited only by launch service provided by the navy. Lines are often long so arrive early in the day. **Sea Life Park**, on the scenic west side of Honolulu, is another worthwhile attraction.

No visit to Oahu would be complete without a trip to the **Polynesian Cultural Center** in Laie. Set on 35 beautifully landscaped, tropical acres, this is an authentic grouping of "villages" representing seven different Polynesian and Micronesian cultures. It is 40 miles from Waikiki by SRs 61 and 83, and you should allocate most of an entire day, including travel time, to see all of it. The scenic 90-minute drive up the coast is an added bonus. Brief stops should be made along the way at the spectacular **Nuuanu Pali State Wayside** (one of the most dramatic vistas in all the islands), and at the **Byodo-In Temple** in the beautiful Valley of the Temples. Sights en route also include the **Chinaman's Hat**, a large rock formation off the coast. At the Polynesian Cultural Center you will see a range of activities taking place in each of the villages and there are several shows and tours during the day – don't miss the Pageant of the Long Canoes. Stay for a delicious buffet dinner and a great evening show. Tickets can be purchased at the center or in Honolulu. The ride back to the city, even at night, is an easy one.

Finally, one of the best ways to see Honolulu is from the two-hour scenic drive on **Roundtop Mountain**. The Roundtop-Tantalus route will take you through dense forests and other areas of great beauty, while offering spectacular views down upon Honolulu and Waikiki.

For More Information

The listings that follow will help you to secure the information needed to make your plans, especially if you are following one of the preceding suggested trips. Addresses and telephone numbers for the national parks themselves are listed in the appropriate chapters.

General information about the nation's natural areas can be obtained from:

>National Park Service
>P.O. Box 37127
>Washington, DC 20013-7127

National Park Service regional offices are located in Boston, Philadelphia, Atlanta, Omaha, Denver, Santa Fe, San Francisco, Seattle and Anchorage. If you live in one of these areas, consult your telephone directory for the local address and telephone number.

All national park camping reservations can be made up to eight weeks in advance through **MISTIX**:

>MSITIX
>P.O. Box 85705
>San Diego CA 92186-5705
>at (800) 365-2267 (CAMP)

State Tourism Offices

Note: Only states with parks mentioned in the book are included in this listing.

ARIZONA
Office of Tourism
1100 W. Washington St.
Phoenix AZ 85007
(602) 255-3618

CALIFORNIA
Office of Tourism
1121 L St., Suite 103
Sacramento CA 95814
(916) 322-1396

COLORADO
Colorado Tourism Board
PO Box 38700
Denver CO 80238
(800) 433-2656

DISTRICT OF COLUMBIA
Washington Visitors Assoc.
1575 Eye St. NW, Suite 250
Washington DC 20005
(202) 789-7000

FLORIDA
Division of Tourism
101 E. Gaines
Tallahassee FL 32399
(904) 487-1462

HAWAII
Hawaii Visitors Bureau
2270 Kalakaua Ave.
Honolulu HI 96815
(808) 923-1811

IDAHO
Idaho Travel Council
707 W. State St.
Boise ID 83720
(800) 635-7820

KENTUCKY
Dept. of Tourism
2200 Capital Plaza Tower
Frankfort KY 40601
(800) 225-8747

MAINE
Maine Publicity
97 Winthrop St.
Hallowell ME 04347
(800) 533-9595

MONTANA
Travel Montana
1424 9th Ave.
Helena MT 59620
(800) 541-1447

NEBRASKA
Travel & Tourism Division
301 Centennial Mall South
PO Box 94666
Lincoln NE 68509
(800) 228-4307

NEVADA
Commission on Tourism
Capitol Complex
Carson City NV 89710
(702) 885-4322

NEW HAMPSHIRE
New Hampshire Vacation Center
PO Box 856
Concord NH 03301
(603) 271-2343

NEW MEXICO
New Mexico Travel Division
100 St. Francis Drive
Santa Fe NM 87503
(800) 545-2040

NEW YORK
Dept. of Commerce
Tourism Division
One Commerce Plaza
Albany NY 12245
(800) 225-5697

OREGON
Oregon Tourism Division
Economic Development Dept.
595 Cottage St. N.E.
Salem OR 97310
(800) 547-7842

TENNESSEE
Dept. of Tourist Development
PO Box 23170
Nashville TN 37202
(615) 741-2158

UTAH
Utah Travel Council
Council Hall/Capitol Hill
Salt Lake City UT 84114
(801) 538-1030

VIRGINIA
Division of Tourism
202 N. 9th St.
Suite 500
Richmond VA 23219
(800) 847-4882

WYOMING
Wyoming Travel Commission
I-25 at College Drive
Cheyenne WY 82002
(800) 225-5996

NORTH CAROLINA
Travel & Tourism
430 N. Salisbury St.
Raleigh NC 27603
(800) 847-4862

SOUTH DAKOTA
Division of Tourism
711 Wells Ave.
Pierre SD 57501
(800) 843-1930

TEXAS
Capitol Info Center
State Hwys & Public
   Transportation Dept.
11th & Brazos Sts.
Austin TX 78701
(512) 462-9191

VERMONT
Vermont Travel Division
Agency of Development &
   Community Affairs
134 State St.
Montpelier VT 05602
(802) 828-3236

WASHINGTON
Trade & Economic Development
Tourism Division
101 General Admin. Bldg.
Olympia WA 98504
(800) 544-1800

Canada

Government Office of Tourism
235 Queen St.
Ottawa, Ontario K1A OH6
(800) 268-3735

Parks Canada
Dept. of the Environment
Ottawa, Ontario K1A OH4
(613) 997-2800

ALBERTA
Travel Alberta
10025 Jasper Ave.
PO Box 2500
Edmonton, Alberta T5J 3Z3
(800) 661-8888

BRITISH COLUMBIA
Ministry of Tourism
Legislative Buildings
Victoria, BC V8V 1X4
(604) 387-1642